The Political Philosophy
of Thomas Jefferson

26.95

THE

POLITICAL PHILOSOPHY OF

Thomas Jefferson

—————————— BY ——————————

GARRETT WARD SHELDON

The Johns Hopkins University Press

Baltimore & London

#22494126

The Johns Hopkins University Press
701 West 40th Street
Baltimore, Maryland 21211
The Johns Hopkins Press Ltd., London

∞ The paper used in this book meets
the minimum requirements of American National Standard
for Information Sciences — Permanence of Paper
for Printed Library Materials,
ANSI Z39.48-1984.

Library of Congress Cataloging-in-Publication Data

Sheldon, Garrett Ward, 1954–
The political philosophy of Thomas Jefferson / Garrett Ward Sheldon.
p.   cm.
Includes bibliographical references and index.
ISBN 0-8018-4142-9
1. Jefferson, Thomas, 1743–1826 — Political and social views.
2. United States — Politics and government — Revolution, 1775–1783.
3. United States — Politics and government — 1783–1809. I. Title.
E332.2.S54   1991   973.4'6'092 — dc20   90-49524

FOR

Cornelia Kellogg Sheldon

AND

Gwendolyn Mary Sheldon

NATURAL ARISTOCRATS BOTH

CONTENTS

PREFACE

As THE AUTHOR of the Declaration of Independence and philosopher of the triumphant Democratic-Republican party,
Thomas Jefferson might be considered the intellectual father of
our country. The range of his intellectual achievements was aptly
characterized by President John F. Kennedy when, at a dinner
celebrating American Nobel laureates, he said that this was "the
most extraordinary collection of talents . . . that has ever been
gathered together at the White House, with the possible exception of when Thomas Jefferson dined alone." That status as the
philosopher of American democracy has rendered the scholarly
assessment of the precise nature of Jefferson's political thought
particularly intense. I hope that this book will contribute more
light than heat to the debate. It does not presume to provide a
final word on the subject and concurs with Merrill Peterson's
belief that Thomas Jefferson "is one of those men about whom
the last word can never be said . . . he demands continual re-
study and re-evaluation."[1] However, I hope that this historical
and theoretical study of Jefferson's political philosophy will provide a starting point for further studies, by clearing the way
through certain dilemmas of current early American historiography.

I gratefully acknowledge the contributions to this work of my
many colleagues, teachers, and friends at Rutgers University,
especially Wilson Carey McWilliams, Benjamin Barber, M. J.
Aronoff, David Rebovich, Richard Battistoni, Laura Greyson,
Bruce Smith, Steven Dworetz, David Schultz, and Judith Grant.

---

[1] Merrill D. Peterson, *Thomas Jefferson and the New Nation* (New York: Oxford
University Press, 1970), p. viii.

Also, Josh Miller at Princeton, Michael Rosano at Toronto, and Chuck Hersch at Berkeley. My colleagues in the University of Virginia, including E. L. Henson, Glenn Blackburn, Joseph M. Scolnick, Jr., Robert Dise, Richard Peake, David Rouse, David Jodrey, Kenneth Thompson, Alexander Sedgwick, and Robert M. O'Neil, offered direct and indirect advice and encouragement, which carries no liability for my own excesses.

Portions of this book, at various stages of development, were presented at academic conferences and benefited from critical comments by participants, including Joseph Knippenberg and Richard Battistoni at the American Political Science Association Conferences in 1986 and 1988, Michael Gillespie and Ruth Grant at the Southern Political Science Association Conferences in 1986 and 1987, Sandra Hinchman at the Southwestern Political Science Association Conference in 1988, and my many colleagues, especially Joseph Freeman, over the years in the Virginia Political Science Association meetings.

This book began as a doctoral dissertation at Rutgers University and, as Carey McWilliams wrote of his *Idea of Fraternity in America,* "to the usual faults of dissertations I have added other defects, nurtured in the intervening years and perfected by revision."[2] Its virtues are largely attributable to those rare manuscript readers who combine rigor with intellectual detachment and sympathy.

I was also fortunate to work with the Executive Editor of the Johns Hopkins University Press, Henry Y. K. Tom, who combined equally rare professional competence and courtesy. Judith Kirkwood's editorial assistance was invaluable. Michael Shortridge, Esq., the leading Jeffersonian of Norton, Virginia, provided valuable insights and support.

Finally, the careful manuscript preparation by Rhonda Stanley and Terry Wells is, as always, deeply appreciated.

---

[2]Wilson Carey McWilliams, *The Idea of Fraternity in America* (Berkeley: University of California Press, 1973), p. i.

CHAPTER 1

LIBERALISM AND
CLASSICISM IN JEFFERSON'S
POLITICAL PHILOSOPHY

GREAT MEN are obliged to suffer many indignities, not the least
of which is the tendency of lesser men continually to write books
about them. Thomas Jefferson has suffered in this regard perhaps
more than any other famous American. Volumes have been written on Jefferson as a lawyer, architect, educator, musician, scientist, social scientist, artist, military strategist, party leader, bib-
liophile, agriculturist, and even as a tourist. In addition to books
affirming Jefferson's character as a Renaissance man, several studies have addressed his political thought, either by itself or within
the context of early American political theory generally.

This book studies the historical development of Thomas Jefferson's political philosophy within the context of the major
themes of Western political theory and the contemporary his-
toriographic debates over early American political thought. An
article by historian J. G. A. Pocock, in which he effectively
launched the "classical republican" paradigm, described three
approaches to the study of past political ideas: (1) the historical
approach, which examines the language used by a society to
discuss political problems; (2) the political science approach,
which studies the role of political language in political activity;
and (3) the approach of political philosophy, which, more ab-

stractly, examines the concepts in past political ideas and their relation to other theories found throughout the history of Western political thought.[1] While most works on Jefferson's political thought use one of the first two approaches as a point of departure, this book employs the third approach, examining the conceptual qualities of Thomas Jefferson's political ideas and relating them to concepts found in the classics of political theory.[2]

This approach reveals that Jefferson's political philosophy was a rich constellation of theoretical qualities from several traditions (British liberalism, classical republicanism, Scottish moral sense philosophy, Christian ethics, and modern economic theory) that changed and evolved as his life passed through the historical periods of America as a colony, revolutionary America, and America as a new republic. Predominantly Lockean in his early, revolutionary writings (especially in the Declaration of Independence), albeit a liberalism adapted to the contingencies of revolutionary colonies seeking independence from a federated empire constructed ideologically from the venerable Ancient Constitution of England, after the Revolution, Jefferson's philosophy assumed a more classical republican quality, complemented by concepts found in Scottish moral sense psychology and basic Christian ethics, and modified by certain aspects of modern economic theory. Later in Jefferson's life, even while expressing a classically "Country" attack on Hamilton and the federal government's "Court" corruption, the Lockean language of rights and independence used during the Revolution against Parliament was again invoked against another remote, centralized regime threatening the sovereign autonomy of small democratic republics—Washington rather than London.

As Gordon Wood has found all early American political thought to be a skein of many strands,[3] so this study finds Jef-

---

[1] J. G. A. Pocock, "Machiavelli, Harrington and English Political Ideologies in the Eighteenth Century," *William and Mary Quarterly* 22 (October 1965): 549–83.

[2] For a more detailed discussion of this methodology, see the introduction to Garrett Ward Sheldon, *The History of Political Theory: Ancient Greece to Modern America* (New York: Peter Lang, 1988).

[3] Gordon Wood, *The Creation of the American Republic* (Chapel Hill: University of North Carolina Press, 1969), pp. 7–29.

ferson blending many philosophical concepts into a comprehensive and coherent political philosophy, the essence of which may be closer to classical republicanism than to Lockean liberalism. Still, Jefferson saw no contradiction between the protection of individual natural rights and popular participation in classical democratic republics; rather, he saw the ongoing and informed participation of democratic citizens as guaranteeing the preservation of basic civil rights. Unlike his colleague, James Madison, who perceived a threat to individual rights from local participatory democracy, Jefferson was sanguine over the possibility of qualified republican deliberation protecting fundamental liberties and therefore was able to blend classical republican and Lockean liberal ideas in his political theory.

Historical scholarship has struggled over the true sources and qualities of American revolutionary and early republican political thought, debating for the last two decades whether the Revolution and founding were premised in Lockean concepts of individualism, natural rights, and limited government, or in the classical republican concepts of Country virtue versus Court corruption, social man, and public participation. (An appendix at the end of the book provides a detailed critique of the past thirty years of historical scholarship.) Jefferson's political philosophy was illuminated by all of these contentions. He was able to accommodate seemingly disparate elements within an original and remarkably coherent worldview to provide a more sophisticated understanding of the ideological foundations of our republic. A summary of the main currents of the last twenty years of historical scholarship on the American Revolution and founding, as well as an examination of the liberal and republican components of Jefferson's conceptions of human nature, political society, and social ethics, follows.

LOCKEAN ORTHODOXY

Until very recently, the American Revolution and founding have been understood solely in terms of the British liberalism of John Locke and related French Enlightenment ideas. Locke's *Second Treatise,* especially, with its conceptions of an isolated, materialist individual in a "state of nature" possessing "natural rights" to life, liberty, and property, establishing a government through a rational "social contract" in order to preserve those private rights and interests through the protection of a strictly limited state, has been seen as the key to prevailing attitudes in the American Revolution and the founding of the United States Constitution.[4] Louis Hartz captured this traditional sense when he wrote in *The Liberal Tradition in America* that "Locke dominates American political thought as no thinker anywhere dominates the political thought of a nation."[5] This Lockean orthodoxy has profoundly affected our appreciation of Thomas Jefferson's political philosophy. Carl Becker's major work on the Declaration of Independence proclaimed that "Jefferson copied Locke."[6] Jefferson's principal biographers, Dumas Malone and Merrill Peterson, also subscribed to this Lockean perspective.[7] Several works devoted to Jefferson's political ideas, including Daniel Boorstin's *The Lost World of Thomas Jefferson*, Gilbert Chinard's *Thomas Jefferson: The Apostle of Americanism*, and Adrienne Koch's *The Philosophy of Thomas Jefferson*, emphasize the liberal and modern Enlightenment ideas in Jefferson's political thought.[8] These books give us the characteristic "Jeffersonian tradition" found in public school textbooks of liberal democracy, individual rights, philosophical materialism and naturalism, religious and economic liberty, and personal freedom.

The Lockean orthodoxy which dominated early American

---

[4] See Sheldon, *The History of Political Theory*, ch. 9.

[5] Louis Hartz, *The Liberal Tradition in America* (New York: Harcourt Brace, 1955), p. 140. See also Isaac Kramnick, "Republican Revisionism Revisited," *American Historical Review* 87 (June 1982): 629–64, at p. 629; and Richard Matthews, *The Radical Politics of Thomas Jefferson* (Lawrence: University Press of Kansas, 1984), pp. 2–5.

[6] Carl Becker, *The Declaration of Independence: A Study in the History of Political Ideas* (New York: Random House, 1958), p. 79.

[7] Dumas Malone, *Jefferson in His Time*, 6 vols. (Boston: Little, Brown, 1948–1981); Merrill D. Peterson, *Thomas Jefferson and the New Nation* (New York: Oxford University Press, 1970).

[8] Daniel Boorstin, *The Lost World of Thomas Jefferson* (New York: Henry Holt, 1948); Gilbert Chinard, *Thomas Jefferson: The Apostle of Americanism* (Boston: Little, Brown, 1929); Adrienne Koch, *The Philosophy of Thomas Jefferson* (Chicago: Quadrangle, 1964).

scholarship for over one hundred years was also congenial with the progressive school of American history found in the works of Charles Beard and Frederick Jackson Turner. Locke's emphasis on private property and conflicting material interests led quite easily into the progressive (and later Marxist) school of historical interpretation that focused upon economic, social, and institutional factors in explaining political ideas and actions in America.

But this Lockean view of American and Jeffersonian thought, which comfortably placed us within a simple, safe, and uniform philosophy of natural rights and limited liberal government, was shattered by a new development in American historiography.

CLASSICAL REPUBLICANISM

Beginning in the 1960s, the classical republican paradigm became what historian Joyce Appleby called "the most protean concept" in early American scholarship.[9] It did this by challenging the Lockean orthodoxy with an alternative ideology that conceived of man as naturally social, with a need to participate in political life and display a capacity for public virtue.[10] This classical republican school of political ideology, largely developed by historian J. G. A. Pocock, is a complex and intricate theoretical formulation drawn from the writings of several nonliberal philosophers, including Aristotle, Cicero, Machiavelli, and James Harrington.[11] It constitutes a body of ideas about man's political

---

[9]Joyce Appleby, "Republicanism and Ideology," *American Quarterly* 37 (Fall 1985): 461–73, at p. 461. Most scholars trace this paradigm back to Z. S. Fink, *The Classical Republicans* (Evanston, Ill.: Northwestern University Press, 1949); and Carolyn Robbins, *The Eighteenth Century Commonwealthsmen* (Cambridge, Mass.: Harvard University Press, 1959).

[10]Robert E. Shalhope, "Republicanism and Early American Historiography," *William and Mary Quarterly* 39 (April 1982): 334–56; John Diggins, *The Lost Soul of American Politics* (New York: Basic Books, 1984), p. 10.

[11]J. G. A. Pocock, *The Machiavellian Moment* (Princeton, N.J.: Princeton University Press, 1969); Pocock, ed., *Three British Revolutions, 1641, 1688, 1776* (Princeton, N.J.: Princeton University Press, 1980); Pocock, *Virtue, Commerce and History* (Cambridge: Cambridge University Press, 1985); Pocock, "Machiavelli, Harrington, and English Political Ideologies."

nature and the just society that moved from Ancient Greece to Rome to Renaissance Italy to eighteenth-century England and finally to America. The primary components of this paradigm are that man's nature is essentially political, requiring an economically independent citizenry that participates directly in common rule, thereby developing and expressing its unique human nature and establishing and maintaining a virtuous republic.[12] Virtue is a decidedly non-Lockean concept because it requires the individual to sacrifice self-interest for the good of the whole society.[13] In its most recent incarnation, classical republicanism appears in eighteenth-century England, where a virtuous Country gentry holds back the decay of the republic that is rapidly being corrupted by a wealthy, decadent Court faction concentrating power and undermining the economic independence of the citizenry with paper money, public credit and debt, stockjobbing, financial imperialism, and standing armies. Such a concentration of wealth, power, and vice, threatening sturdy, frugal republican virtue, can only be resisted by returning to the original principles of the English Ancient Constitution, which respect the virtue and independence of the common citizen and the traditional balance of the mixed English Constitution.[14]

This ideology came to America when the colonists perceived the acts of Parliament in the 1760s to be a reassertion of Court corruption and the Revolution as preserving the republican virtues of honest civil government.[15] So, the American Revolution was not a struggle for Lockean rights and limited liberal government, but a nostalgic battle for the preservation of original

---

[12] See esp. Pocock, *The Machiavellian Moment,* pp. 66–68.

[13] J. G. A. Pocock, "Cambridge Paradigms and Scotch Philosophers," in *Wealth and Virtue,* eds. Istvan Hont and Michael Ignatieff (Cambridge: Cambridge University Press, 1983), pp. 235–37.

[14] Fink, *The Classical Republicans*; Pocock, *The Machiavellian Moment,* pp. 407–552; Pocock, *Three British Revolutions,* pp. 5–14; Pocock, *Virtue, Commerce and History,* pp. 74–87; Joyce Appleby, "Republicanism in Old and New Contexts," *William and Mary Quarterly* 43 (January 1986): 20–34; Appleby, "Republicanism and Ideology"; Wood, *The Creation of the American Republic,* ch. 2.

[15] Pocock, *Three British Revolutions,* pp. 13–14; Bernard Bailyn, *The Ideological Origins of the American Revolution* (Cambridge, Mass.: Harvard University Press, 1967), pp. 48–50; Pocock, *Virtue, Commerce and History.*

republican principles threatened by a corrupt, financial empire. Thus, for J. G. A. Pocock, the Revolution is not the first act in a modern liberal age, but "the last act of the civic Renaissance."[16] Well, not quite the *last* act. According to the classical republican paradigm, Court corruption raised its ugly head once again when Alexander Hamilton and other Federalists tried to centralize power in the national capitol around a National Bank, manufacturers, financial imperialism, and all the rest, attempting to crush the native agrarian virtue that Jefferson and his party struggled to protect—and ultimately preserve.[17]

The gist of all this is that the American Revolution and founding were not Lockean, but republican; Americans' philosophical roots are not modern, liberal individualism, materialism, progress, freedom, and rights, but rather, ancient, social, spiritual, nostalgic public virtue. But, republican ideology remains a diverse and somewhat vague paradigm, within which scholars disagree over the specific components and extent of its influence.[18]

ASPECTS OF LIBERALISM AND CLASSICISM IN JEFFERSON'S POLITICAL THOUGHT

Thomas Jefferson's political philosophy contains both British liberal and classical republican qualities.[19] Given their widely divergent conceptions of human nature, politics, and ethics, the presence of both schools of thought in Jefferson's philosophy has led to difficulties in understanding the nature of Jeffersonian democratic theory. Scholars have argued persuasively that Jef-

---

[16] Pocock, *The Machiavellian Moment*, p. 462.

[17] Ibid., pp. 525–33.

[18] Appleby, "Republicanism in Old and New Contexts," p. 21; Shalhope, "Republicanism and Early American Historiography," p. 335.

[19] By British liberal I mean primarily the political philosophies of Thomas Hobbes and John Locke; by classical republican I mean the political philosophies of Aristotle, Cicero, Montesquieu, and James Harrington. While significant differences exist among thinkers within each tradition, for purposes of this analysis I will concentrate on the major distinctions between liberalism and classicism. See appendix for further explanation.

7

ferson's political ideas were purely Lockean or purely Aristotelean, citing convincing evidence from Jefferson's own writings. By distinguishing between classical and liberal conceptions of human nature, political society, and social ethics, and by showing how Jefferson's thought at different times reflected each, one can establish the basis for a detailed historical analysis of the development of Jefferson's political philosophy in which those differences dissolve into a consistent and comprehensive worldview.

Human Nature

Classical Greek political thought conceived of man as a naturally social and political being. Aristotle declared that "man is by nature a political animal. . . . Men have a natural desire for life in society."[20] Aristotle distinguished man, who is *political*, from merely gregarious *social* creatures (such as bees or ants) by mankind's capacity for "reasoned speech."[21] But he also insisted that "the real difference between men and other animals is that humans alone have perception of good and evil, right and wrong, just and unjust."[22] These unique faculties of reasoned speech and moral choice render humans naturally social and political, as neither can be either developed or exercised in isolation; they make political society at once possible and necessary. And, as classical political philosophy regards these distinctive human faculties as the highest qualities in man, the political deliberation that develops and refines those faculties becomes man's noblest pursuit—cultivating his distinctive *telos* and creating a virtuous polity. As J. G. A. Pocock has shown, such development, for Aristotle, involved both moral and material preconditions. Aristotle's citizen must possess the economic independence ena-

---

[20] Aristotle, *The Politics,* trans. T. A. Sinclair (Baltimore: Penguin, 1972), book 1, ch. 2, p. 28, book 3, ch. 6, p. 114.

[21] Ibid., book 1, ch. 2, p. 28.

[22] Ibid., p. 29. Aristotle included the human affections as another source of man's natural propensity for society: "for it is our love of others that causes us to prefer life in a society, and they all contribute toward that good life which is the purpose of the state" (book 3, ch. 9, p. 121).

bling him to freely enter the public realm on an equal basis with his fellow citizens.[23]

Modern, liberal political philosophy conceives of man as naturally individual and independent. John Locke declared that man in his natural state is "free, equal, and independent."[24] This free and separate condition derives from liberalism's conception of man as essentially a material being, ruled by the private senses which he shares with no one, guided by the pleasures and pains of this world, and motivated primarily by a desire for continued life, or "self-preservation." And such material existence gives the natural right to those things ("life, liberty, and property") which insure that continued existence. The power of reason is employed by man to best secure those individual rights and that self-preservation. Man's rational faculties do not form an inevitable social bond, as much as the means to create a government that secures his individual freedom and independence.

Thomas Jefferson's conception of man's nature appears quite liberal in his most famous document, the Declaration of Independence: "We hold these truths to be sacred and undeniable; that all men are created equal and independent, that from that creation they derive rights inherent and inalienable, among which are the preservation of life, and liberty, and the pursuit of happiness."[25] Yet elsewhere, Jefferson's view of the human psyche seems decidedly classical. He declared in various letters that man is "an animal destined to live in society," because "the Creator . . . intended man for a social animal."[26] He specifically criticized

---

[23] Pocock, *The Machiavellian Moment*, pp. 66–68; Aristotle, *Politics*, book 3, ch. 9.

[24] John Locke, *Two Treatises of Government*, ed. Peter Laslett (New York: New American Library, 1965).

[25] From Jefferson's "original Rough draught," prior to Committee revisions, *The Papers of Thomas Jefferson*, 60 vols., ed. Julian Boyd (Princeton, N.J.: Princeton University Press, 1950), 1: 423–27, hereafter *Papers*. Much has been made of Jefferson's substitution of "pursuit of happiness" for Locke's "prosperity," or "estate." My argument that Jefferson's use of "happiness" reflects his Aristotelean bent, as seen as the ultimate end of human life in Aristotle's *Nicomachean Ethics*, book 1, trans. Martin Ostwald (Indianapolis: Bobbs-Merrill 1962), is elaborated in ch. 3.

[26] Jefferson to John Adams, October 14, 1816, *The Adams-Jefferson Letters*, 2

Hobbes's psychology (calling it a "humiliation to human nature")[27] and offered an alternative syllogism echoing Aristotle's conception of a naturally social and ethical humanity: "Man was created for social intercourse; but social intercourse cannot be maintained without a sense of justice; then man must have been created with a sense of justice."[28] Indeed, on several occasions Jefferson seemed more inclined to ascribe some error on God's part than to admit that man is not naturally a social and ethical being: "The Creator would have been a bungling artist, had he intended man for a social animal, without planting in him social dispositions."[29]

Political Society

Corresponding to its vision of human nature as consisting of free, equal and independent individuals possessing natural rights to life, liberty and property, modern liberalism conceives of politics as consisting of a limited state of delegated authority charged with preserving those individual rights. For Locke, if all men were rationally self-interested and capable of respecting others' rights, no state would be necessary at all. But because some men violate the rights of others by threatening their lives or property, a government is instituted, by the consent of the governed, to secure the natural rights of individuals from invasion by others:

> To avoid, and remedy these inconveniences of the State of Nature
> . . . Men join and unite into a community, for their comfortable,

---

vols., ed. Lester J. Cappon (Chapel Hill: University of North Carolina Press, 1959), 2: 492, hereafter *A-JL*; to Peter Carr, August 10, 1787, *The Writings of Thomas Jefferson,* 20 vols., ed. Albert Ellery Bergh (Washington D.C.: Thomas Jefferson Memorial Association, 1904–1905), 6: 257, hereafter *WTJ*; also see to Thomas Law, June 13, 1814, *The Complete Jefferson,* ed. Saul K. Padover (New York: Tudor, 1943), p. 1033, hereafter *CJ.*

[27] Jefferson to Francis Gilmer, June 7, 1816, *WTJ,* 15: 24.

[28] Ibid., p. 25.

[29] Jefferson to Thomas Law, June 13, 1814, *CJ,* p. 1033. See also Jefferson to Peter Carr, August 10, 1787, *WTJ,* 6: 257 ("He who made us would have been a pitiful bungler . . ."); and to John Adams, October 14, 1816, in *A-JL,* 2: 492 ("as a wise creator must have seen to be necessary in an animal destined to live in society").

safe and peaceful living one amongst another, in a secure Enjoyment of their Properties, and a greater Security against any that are not of it. . . . The great and chief end of Mens uniting into Commonwealths and putting themselves under Government, *is the Preservation of their Property.*[30]

And because this government is established by free individuals and limited to preserving their natural rights, if it ever ceases to perform its function (or worse, invades the peoples' rights itself), those individuals that formed it may dissolve the government and establish one that will properly serve their interests. Such dissolution of government constitutes Locke's famous right to revolution: "When the Arbitrary Power of the Prince, the Electors, or ways of Election are altered, without the Consent, and contrary to the common Interest of the People, there . . . the Legislative is altered [and] the People are at Liberty to provide for themselves by erecting a new Legislative."[31]

In contrast to Locke's conception of the state as limited to preserving individual rights, the ancients conceived of politics as cultivating man's highest faculties and establishing a polity of virtue and purpose. Aristotle maintained that man is naturally a social being, born with the capacity for reasoned speech and moral choice, but he also insisted that those attributes be cultivated and refined: "virtues are implanted in us neither by nature nor contrary to nature: we are by nature equipped with the ability to receive them, and habit brings this ability to completion and fulfillment. . . . we are provided with the capacity [*dynamis*: potential] first, and display the activity [*energia*: actuality] afterward."[32] And the best way in which to develop man's social faculties is through direct participation in the politics of a small democratic society: "the state cannot be defined merely as a community dwelling in the same place and preventing its members from wrongdoing and promoting the exchange of goods and services. . . . [rather, politics should] engender a certain

---

[30] Locke, *Two Treatises,* ch. 7, p. 369, ch. 8, p. 375, ch. 9, p. 395.
[31] Ibid., ch. 19, pp. 457, 459.
[32] Aristotle, *Nicomachean Ethics,* book 2, 1103a, p. 33; see also book 2, 1103a–1103b, p. 33–34 ("virtues . . . we acquire by first having to put them into action . . . we learn by doing . . . we become just by the practice of just actions").

character in the citizens and make them good and disposed to perform noble actions."[33]

Thus, Aristotle's notion of citizenship implies the direct participation in local politics, which cultivates man's social and ethical faculties: "A citizen is in general one who has a share both in ruling and in being ruled with a view of life that is in accordance with goodness."[34] Such direct citizen participation in political affairs necessitates a small democracy, like the Greek polis, where everyone knows his fellow citizens: "In order to give decisions on matters of justice and for the purpose of distributing offices in accordance with the work of the applicants, it is necessary that the citizens should know each other and know what kind of people they are."[35] A liberal state limited to protecting private rights may easily be a vast representative democracy; but a classical republic that seeks to cultivate man's social faculties, which conceives of a "public" realm apart from private interest, requires small participatory democracy, and an economically independent citizenry.[36]

Thomas Jefferson's conception of politics seems at times to reflect the liberal, social contract view of a limited government devoted to preserving private rights. Again, this perspective appears in the Declaration of Independence: "to secure these ends, governments are instituted among men, deriving their just powers from the consent of the governed, [and] whenever any form of government shall become destructive of these ends, it is the right of the people to alter or to abolish it and to institute new government."[37] This liberal view is also found in Jefferson's writings respecting the federal government, as evidenced in his first

---

[33] Aristotle, *Politics,* book 3, ch. 9, p. 120; and Aristotle, *Nicomachean Ethics,* book 1, 1099b, p. 23.

[34] Aristotle, *Politics,* book 3, ch. 13, pp. 131–32; see also book 3, ch. 1, p. 102 ("What effectively distinguishes the citizen from all others is his participation in Judgement and Authority, that is, holding office, legal, political, administrative"); and book 3, ch. 4, p. 112 ("There are different kinds of citizens, but . . . a citizen in the fullest sense is one who has a share in the privileges of rule").

[35] Ibid., book 7, ch. 4, p. 266.

[36] Ibid., book 1, ch. 8, book 3, chs. 4, 9; Pocock, *The Machiavellian Moment,* pp. 66–68.

[37] Jefferson, *Papers,* 1: 423–27.

inaugural address: "[America requires] a wise and frugal government, which shall restrain men from injuring one another, which shall leave them otherwise free to regulate their own pursuits of industry and improvement."[38]

Yet much of Jefferson's writings concerning American democracy seem to advocate small participatory republics, cultivating man's innate social faculties and establishing a virtuous polity. Jefferson's extensive efforts in dividing the Virginia counties into wards of five to six square miles and one hundred citizens for educational, economic, and political purposes reveal strongly classical sympathies: "Each ward would thus be a small republic within itself, and every man in the state would thus become an acting member of the common government, transacting in person a great portion of its rights and duties . . . entirely within his competence. The wit of man cannot devise a more solid basis for a free, durable and well-administered republic."[39] Elsewhere, Jefferson indicated that without such citizen participation in the virtuous republic, leaders would turn into "wolves" and the people would be reduced to "mere automatons of misery, to have no sensibilities but for sinning and suffering."[40] Thus, with respect to his efforts to amend Virginia's constitution dividing the counties into small ward republics, Jefferson wrote: "Could I once see this I should consider it as the dawn of the salvation of the republic, and say with old Simeon, '*nunc dimittis Domine.*' "[41]

Social Ethics

Lockean social ethics are essentially negative by virtue of their moral imperative to not harm others, to refrain from infringing upon others' rights and freedom, allowing them to pursue their

---

[38]Thomas Jefferson, "First Inaugural Address," *CJ,* p. 386.
[39]Jefferson to Major John Cartwright, June 5, 1824, *WTJ,* 16: 46. Note also Jefferson's last remark to Monsieur Coray that "Greece was the first of civilized nations which presented examples of what man should be" (*WTJ,* 15: 480–90).
[40]Jefferson to Col. Edward Carrington, January 16, 1787, ibid., 5: 58, and to Samuel Kercheval, July 12, 1816, 15: 40.
[41]Jefferson to Gov. John Tyler, May 26, 1810, ibid., 12: 394.

own interests in ways that they see fit. Individuals, society, and the state are obliged to respect the rights of individuals, especially as they relate to the individual's pursuit of his own self-interest (or self-preservation) and the life, liberty, and property necessary to that pursuit. Conservative, laissez-faire economics, with its emphasis on leaving the market forces free to regulate themselves, without political interference, corresponds nicely with these negative liberal ethics.[42] Their political ascension is usually marked by the formal separation of ethics and politics, or church and state.

The origins of such ethics reside in the epistemology emerging from modern empiricism, which relies on individual sensory perception as the sole source of knowledge. For, if no unified truth can emerge from the diversity of perceptions, no one is justified in prescribing moral lessons to others; the autonomous perception and judgment of the individual must be respected. No objective standards can exist above subjective choice, given such epistemological relativism. The one area where liberal psychology can legislate is with regard to material harm and loss, or violations of individuals' rights and freedom. Therefore, liberal social ethics are confined to restraining and punishing violence and theft (the state *qua* police), but otherwise leave individuals free to their own devices.

Classical social ethics are positive in the sense that they insist that it is not enough to merely refrain from injuring others; moral action requires an effort to improve others, encouraging the perfection of their souls. As Aristotle maintains that happiness comes from possessing a virtuous character, individuals are obliged to cultivate the highest goodness in others.[43] Socrates's rebuttal of Meletus's charge of corrupting the Athenean youth (that one is made better or worse by the quality of one's associates,

---

[42] For this reason, along with Locke's justification for the unlimited accumulation of property, C. B. Macpherson considers them the ethics of bourgeois individualism and capitalist social relations, see *The Political Theory of Possessive Individualism: Hobbes to Locke* (Oxford: Clarendon Press, 1962); *Democratic Theory* (Oxford: Clarendon Press, 1973), p. 228–33; and *The Life and Times of Liberal Democracy* (Oxford: Oxford University Press, 1977), p. 22.

[43] Aristotle, *Nicomachean Ethics*, books 9, 10.

making deliberate corruption of others harmful to oneself) commends an ethics which ties one's own goodness and happiness to those around one, and obliges one to cultivate others' goodness.[44] But such ethics imply an objective standard—revealed by God or determined collectively—that transcends individual perception and interest. Perhaps the best statement of these classical social ethics (which re-emerge in Christian ethics) is that made by Socrates at his trial after receiving the sentence of death:

> When my sons grow up, gentlemen, if you think they are putting money or anything else before goodness, take your revenge by plaguing them as I plagued you; and if they fancy themselves for no reason, you must scold them just as I have scolded you, for neglecting the important things and thinking that they are good for something when they are good for nothing. If you do this, I shall have had justice at your hands.[45]

Thomas Jefferson's social ethics reveal a liberal inclination in his attack on the established Church of England and in his advocacy of the separation of church and state and the corollary right to religious freedom.[46] Yet, as we shall see, Jefferson's advocacy of religious freedom did not derive so much from an epistemological skepticism as from the hope that through the free expression of all religious denominations, the people might distill those simple teachings of Jesus that Jefferson considered the one true religion. His preference for Christian ethics also derived from his belief that they were the most advanced social ethics or morals governing human relations, and so most suited to a naturally social being and the most social of regimes—participatory democracy.

Jefferson's personal ethics also revealed a liberal reluctance to force his moral views on others, as he expressed in a letter to his grandson: "I never saw an instance of one or two disputants convincing the other by argument. [But] I have seen many, on

---

[44] Plato's *Apology*, *The Last Days of Socrates*, trans. Hugh Tredennick (Baltimore: Penguin, 1954), pp. 70–74.

[45] Ibid., p. 76.

[46] Thomas Jefferson, The Bill for Establishing Religious Freedom (1779), *CJ*, p. 946.

their getting warm, becoming rude, and shooting one another."[47] Instead of preaching to others, Jefferson encouraged "asking questions, as if for information, or suggesting doubts."[48] This seems mild, indeed, but it was also the method of Socrates and Jesus.[49]

JEFFERSON'S EVOLVING POLITICAL PHILOSOPHY

Jefferson was Lockean during the revolutionary period, especially in the Declaration of Independence, albeit a Lockean modified by the contingencies of a revolutionary colonist, within a federated empire constructed out of ideas in the Ancient Constitution. It is in this way that the free, equal, and independent men of Locke's state of nature become the free, equal and independent legislatures of Jefferson's British Empire. Such modified liberalism reappears in Jefferson's later writings against Hamilton's Federalists and Marshall's Court, again defending the autonomy of independent democratic communities against oppression from a distant, centralized, and corrupt regime. Jefferson's republican Country ideology is clearly expressed here as his conception of the mixed constitution is of the national (one), states (few), and the counties and wards (many), unbalanced by the Court shifting all power to the central government.

Looking at the kind of democratic community that Jefferson so assiduously defended with Lockean concepts, we find a more classical republican vision of economically independent, educated citizens participating directly in the common rule of local ward republics. This classical political order is premised on a naturally social human nature emanating from a moral sense and refined with Christian ethics. And yet, we find that this classical republic in Jefferson's mind is not incompatible with individual freedom

---

[47]Jefferson to Thomas Jefferson Randolph, November 24, 1808, *WTJ*, 12: 196–202.

[48]Ibid., p. 199.

[49]See Plato's Socratic Dialogues, esp. *Crito, Euthyphro, Gorgias, Protagoras, Meno,* book 1 of *The Republic;* and *The Gospels,* esp. *Matthew* 22:41–45; *Mark* 7:1–24; *Luke* 20:1–9; and *John* 18:33–39.

and certain kinds of economic developments, but could actually benefit in an Aristotelean self-sufficiency through such freedom and development.

Jefferson actually combines liberalism and republicanism in his political philosophy in two ways. Although each predominates at different historical periods (the Lockean during the revolutionary and the anti-Federalist periods and the republican during the postrevolutionary construction period), both are present at all times. Lockean liberalism predominates against the Parliament and the Federalists to defend autonomous republic legislatures in the colonies and the states; and the classical republics in ward, county, state, and national governments, protect, in Jefferson's view, individual rights and liberties from tyrannical government.

Finally, we find that Jefferson embodied certain traditional landed values through his participation in the culture of the Virginia gentry, although this "Tory" character affected his personal manners and style more than his political beliefs. As Rhys Isaac has shown, Jefferson sought to replace the traditional hierarchical society and hereditary aristocracy with a hierarchy of republican regimes and an aristocracy of merit and virtue.[50]

This study examines the ideological context of the British Empire into which Jefferson was born, an imperial realm settling colonies in America under an absolute monarch bound by feudal traditions and charters, yet later expanded by a commercially-minded Parliament, while retaining ideological elements of the Crown. It shows how Jefferson's legal studies imbued him with principles generated by the English political turmoils of 1660 to 1688, especially the Ancient Constitution and Locke's natural rights philosophy, which he adapted in his ideological struggles for colonial independence; and analyzes his postrevolutionary political philosophy, in his conceptions of human nature, political society, and social ethics, along with related views on education,

---

[50]Rhys Isaac, *The Transformation of Virginia 1740–1790* (Chapel Hill: University of North Carolina Press, 1982), pp. 294–95. See also Melvin Yazawa, *From Colonies to Commonwealth: Familial Ideology and the Beginnings of the American Republic* (Baltimore: Johns Hopkins University Press, 1985), pp. 35–36, 131–32, 168; and A. G. Roeber, *Faithful Magistrates and Republican Lawyers* (Chapel Hill: University of North Carolina Press, 1981), pp. 163–68, 239.

economics, religion, federalism, and aristocracy. It considers the culture of the Virginia gentry, which affected Jefferson's personal tastes and style, and the shadow which the slavery of that culture cast over his political ideals. It concludes with a reexamination of theoretical concepts often associated with Jefferson (freedom, rights, equality, and democracy) from the perspective of the development of his political philosophy, and with a brief discussion of Jefferson as a political philosopher, the effects of the varied historical, social, and philosophical influences on his thought and how they combined to produce his unique perspective.

CHAPTER 2

AMERICA AS A COLONY: THE BRITISH

REALM VERSUS JEFFERSON'S

MODERN EMPIRE

THOMAS JEFFERSON approached the American Revolution with fear, anguish, and resolve: fear of the treason his acts implied and the early death it promised; anguish over the separation from traditional ties with Great Britain; yet resolve to carry through his duty for independence despite the political dangers and personal grief.[1]

In the years immediately prior to the Revolution, Jefferson became increasingly interested in matters relating to treason and death. The journal into which he copied notes and quotations from various legal and philosophical studies reveals a profound interest in English treason: its origins in allegiance, the determination of its limits, any exceptions to its purview, and the penalties following from its conviction.[2] From Sir Edward Coke's

---

[1] Much of Jefferson's emotional response to separation with the "mother country" can be explained by the dominant familial model of society and politics in the British Empire, as shown by Melvin Yazawa, *From Colonies to Commonwealth: Familial Ideology and the Beginnings of the American Republic* (Baltimore: Johns Hopkins University Press, 1985), esp. pp. 2–4, 85–112.

[2] Thomas Jefferson, *The Commonplace Book of Thomas Jefferson: A Repertory of His Ideas on Government,* ed. Gilbert Chinard (Baltimore: Johns Hopkins Press, 1926), entries 29–46, 242.

Institutes of the Laws of England (1671), Jefferson learned that treasonable offenses committed in other royal dominions (notably Ireland) had been tried in England, that in cases involving high treason (attempts to alter the fundamental laws of the realm) *all* participants were considered principals (none mere accomplices), and that conviction invariably led to the loss of life and lands.[3]

It is not surprising, then, that the subject of death came to occupy much of Jefferson's thought during the years preceding his revolutionary acts. His journal of literature and poetry during this time contains quotations concerning death from no fewer than twelve authors, ancient and modern (Herodotus, Cicero, Euripides, Homer, Horace, Pope, Samuel Butler, Milton, Young, Shakespeare, Fryar, and Manilius).[4] These literary depictions are not limited to expressions of private despondency by a jilted lover or bereaved son (for Jefferson at this time was both); rather, they display sentiments of political daring and public execution. Specifically, in Jefferson's extractions from Cicero, we find the belief that dying in a just cause constitutes answering God's call and following in the footsteps of Socrates and Cato: "For that God who presides in us forbids our departure hence without his leave. But when God himself has given us a just cause, as formerly he did to Socrates, and late to Cato . . . certainly every man of sense would gladly exchange this darkness for that light."[5] From Euripides, Jefferson learned of the satisfaction attending an honorable death: "As for a tomb I would wish mine to be one that men, seeing, honor; long enduring is that satisfaction."[6] And from Homer, that the most honorable death is one suffered in the service of one's country:

> Death is the worst; a Fate which all must try;
> And, for our Country, 'tis a Bliss to die,
> The gallant Man tho' slain in Fight he be,

---

[3]Ibid., entries 31, 35, 41, 46.
[4]Thomas Jefferson, *The Literary Bible of Thomas Jefferson: His Commonplace Book of Philosophers and Poets,* intro. Gilbert Chinard (Baltimore: Johns Hopkins Press, 1928).
[5]Ibid., pp. 74–75.
[6]Ibid., pp. 82–83.

Yet leaves his Nation safe, his children free,
Entails a debt on all the grateful State;
His own brave Friends shall glory in his Fate;
His wife live Honour'd, all his Race succeed;
And late Posterity enjoy the Deed.[7]

Such abundant incentive for heroic sacrifice strengthened Jefferson's resolve against the fear of treason's punishment, and, if that were not enough, he took warning from Shakespeare over the punishment of cowardice:

Cowards die many Times before their Deaths;
The valient never taste Death but once.[8]

Despite his concern over treason and death, and his attempts to overcome that fear through honorable service to his country's cause, Jefferson's early writings also evince a profound anguish over separating from the British Empire. This separation from the affectionate ties of allegiance to America's mother country was a kind of death itself, revealing the familial ties engendered by the original English settlement.[9] In his *Summary View of the Rights of British America* (1774), considered a very radical pamphlet at the time, Jefferson beseeches the king to restore "fraternal love and harmony thro' the whole empire," securing a "well-poised empire" of harmony and reciprocity.[10] And even in his overtly revolutionary tract, *The Declaration of the Causes and Necessity for Taking Up Arms* (1775), Jefferson attributes the colonies' prior toleration of Parliament's incursions into their affairs to the "warmth of affection" between America and "Mother England."[11] Similarly, Jefferson wrote to John Randolph of the "unnatural contest" ensuing between the colonies

---

[7] Pope's translation, ibid., p. 127.
[8] Ibid., p. 147.
[9] Garry Wills inappropriately ascribes Jefferson's sentiments to his intellectual adherence to the Scottish moral sense school (and its doctrine of human sympathy)—see *Inventing America: Jefferson's Declaration of Independence* (New York: Doubleday, 1978), p. 291. Actually, the sources of Jefferson's anguish are historical and cultural—see Yazawa, *From Colonies to Commonwealth*, p. 87.
[10] Thomas Jefferson, *The Papers of Thomas Jefferson*, 20 vols., ed. Julian Boyd (Princeton, N.J.: Princeton University Press, 1950), 1: 135.
[11] Ibid., p. 199.

and Britain, to which he was "looking with fondness towards a reconciliation."[12]

It was only when those affectionate ties to Britain were stretched beyond endurance and Jefferson was forced to sever all allegiance with the realm that his full anguish over the breach was felt. This occurred when the Crown made war on the colonies, when Britain chose to enforce its dictates not merely with the established forms of rule or even indigenous English soldiers, but with "Scotch and foreign mercenaries."[13] This, for Jefferson, provided "the last stab to agonizing affection," bidding him to "renounce forever these unfeeling brethren" and to advise his fellows to "forget our former love for them."[14]

THE IDEOLOGY OF THE BRITISH EMPIRE

Those strongly emotional and at times conflicting sentiments that Jefferson and other American revolutionaries expressed over separation from Britain derived in part from the prevailing imperial ideology and the changes that had occurred in the British Empire since the original settlements under Elizabeth I. The English colonies in America had originally been settled in the seventeenth century under a feudal monarch and were governed by an ideology and within a structure appropriate to royal dominions. That ideology conceived of a realm that integrated politics, economics, society, and religion into an organic whole ruled by a single sovereign under God's natural law. This vision of a traditional realm was simply extended to the vast British Empire, including colonies within an integral dependency premised in royal allegiance and feudal tenure. Sir Francis Drake conducted his naval adventures and acquired colonial possessions in the name of his queen; Charles I proclaimed Virginia part of the royal empire.

The formal political structure of the American colonies rep-

---

[12]Ibid., p. 241.

[13]In Jefferson's Declaration of Independence, ibid., p. 427.

[14]Ibid., p. 427. For examples of this response in other American colonists, see Yazawa, *From Colonies to Commonwealth,* pp. 85, 94–96.

resented this essentially monarchical feudal order. The Crown's control over colonial politics was ubiquitous. Legitimate territorial existence was granted by royal charters; ruling colonial officials (governor and council) were appointed by the Crown; laws enacted by inferior public assemblies were sent back to London for the king's approval and then returned as royal decrees. The actual gravitation of political authority to the popular colonial assemblies did nothing to alter this formal imperial structure.

The position that the American colonists found themselves in, as distant members of a traditional organic realm, accounted for much of their feelings of both affection for, and resentment of, the royal British Empire. To complicate matters further, the English themselves were increasingly uncomfortable with that traditional monarchical ideology, and after the Glorious Revolution of 1688 and the establishment of parliamentary supremacy, the royal and feudal ideology was retained only as a kind of romantic fiction, which caused an equally dramatic change in imperial relations. For, as sovereignty in England shifted from the Crown to Parliament, the British Empire became increasingly commercial as the merchant class became more influential in Parliament. And as mercantilist interests grew the former conduct of the old empire diminished: in place of expansion for the honor and virtue of the royal sovereign and his realm, the empire grew for purely commercial purposes; in place of integral dependencies within the royal "family" of states, the colonies became objects of purely economic concern.[15] Yet while Parliament and its commercial interests assumed control of the empire, they retained the benign royal ideology which originally established it.[16] This infusion of

---

[15] J. Holland Rose, A. P. Newton, and E. A. Benians, eds., *Cambridge History of the British Empire*, (Cambridge: Cambridge University Press, 1929), pp. 207, 214, 614, 622; Klaus E. Knorr, *British Colonial Theories, 1570–1850* (Toronto: University of Toronto Press, 1944); Richard Koebner, *Empire* (Cambridge: Cambridge University Press, 1961), pp. 9–10.

[16] See Lord Mansfield's speech concerning parliamentary sovereignty in England and in the empire in David C. Douglass, ed., *English Historical Documents*, 12 vols. (Oxford: Oxford University Press, 1950–1968), 10: 753. Members of the Massachusetts Assembly wryly noted this contradiction when replying to the royal governor's insistence that they abide by parliamentary dictums as an obe-

essentially commercial conduct in the robes of traditional ideology certainly contributed to the colonists' confusion and resentment, and fueled their desire for independence.[17]

That desire was given means of theoretical expression by the very ideas that English parliamentarians used to topple the monarchy. For, as we shall see in Jefferson's revolutionary writings, the Ancient Constitution and liberal natural rights philosophy, used so effectively by the English in their ideological battles with the Crown, came back to haunt them one hundred years later when the American colonists used the same approach to destroy the last vestige of royal supremacy: the traditional ideology of the royal British empire. Theories of a virtuous Ancient Constitution and inherent natural rights could not be enshrined in British politics and law without eventually finding their way across the ocean—especially to the growing class of colonial lawyers.[18] Armed with these theories, the American revolutionaries faced an imperial ideology which strangely mixed royal sovereignty based in feudal tenure and parliamentary supremacy pursuing mercantilist policies. Thomas Jefferson became the exemplary revolutionary theorist as he skillfully invoked the leading philosophical arguments for American independence within the labyrinth of British imperial politics and ideology.

---

dient royal colony: "It is necessary for us to inquire how it appears, for your Excellency has not shown it to us, that when, or at that time that our predecessors took possession of this plantation, or colony, under a grant and charter from the Crown of England, it was their sense, and the sense of England, that they were to remain subject to the authority of Parliament" (in James Hosmer, *Life of Thomas Hutchinson, Royal Governor of the Province of Massachusetts Bay,* 1896; New York: Da Capo Press, 1972, p. 382).

[17] See Bernard Bailyn's award-winning book, *The Ideological Origins of the American Revolution* (Cambridge, Mass.: Harvard University Press, 1967). The best attempt to theoretically reconcile this new situation came from Burke's "imperial Parliament"; see his parliamentary speeches in *English Historical Documents,* 10: 758–60. Most British historians acknowledge the damage caused by turning the empire into a purely economic enterprise; see Rose, Newton, and Benians, *Cambridge History,* pp. 605, 622, 626, 613–14.

[18] Note how many notable revolutionary thinkers were trained as English lawyers. For a good discussion of the role they played in Virginia during the colonial and revolutionary periods, see A. G. Roeber, *Faithful Magistrates and Republican Lawyers* (Chapel Hill: University of North Carolina Press, 1981).

Jefferson's revolutionary theories drew more upon the English revolutionary ideas of 1660 to 1688 than upon the classical republican reaction to Walpole's commercialism of 1690 to 1740, as Pocock asserts. Whether the English political ideas affecting the American Revolution were one hundred years old or seventy years old, in this case, means more than just thirty years. If they were drawn from the period culminating in the Glorious Revolution, they would be those essentially antimonarchical, antiauthoritarian theories in the supposed Ancient Constitution and John Locke's *Second Treatise*. If they were from the later period, when Parliament and commercialism were firmly established, they could reasonably be considered the nostalgic Tory republicanism that Pocock describes. This raises the interesting question of how long, in the seventeenth and eighteenth centuries, it took major political ideas to travel across the Atlantic and become firmly planted in the colonial mind. I believe that it took longer than the thirty to eighty years required for the classical republican thesis and that Jefferson, with the other American revolutionaries, was more attuned to the English theories leading to the Glorious Revolution of 1688, namely, Lockean liberalism.

THE ANCIENT CONSTITUTION
AND JEFFERSON'S MODERN EMPIRE

Thomas Jefferson drew upon two common theoretical justifications for American independence: (1) the Ancient Constitution, whose venerable Saxon liberties provided historical precedent for colonial rights; and (2) Lockean liberalism, whose abstract principles of natural right legitimated colonial claims through suprahistorical nature itself. To both of these arguments for American independence, Jefferson brought an unusual breadth and depth of knowledge, acquired from studies extending through the classics in both fields of thought. His understanding of the Ancient Constitution was not limited to the common purveyors of that myth, but included the entire common law tradition of English jurisprudence; his debt to the liberal heritage of John Locke (lately called into question)[19] is not only evident, but extraordinarily clear and learned. Still, Jefferson's use of the Ancient Constitution and Lockean natural rights philosophy must be understood in their place: both were used to corroborate the arguments of revolutionary colonies wishing independence from a traditional empire which had been corrupted with parliamentary mercantilism. Yet, even when Jefferson attacked the corruption of parliamentary politics and commercialism, he did not invoke the classical republican language of virtue, but the rights of the Ancient Constitution. In the process of transplanting these venerable truths to American shores, he formulated an original, federated conception of the British Empire.

In England, the Ancient Constitution consisted of that "perfect liberty" embodied in the principles and practices of government in the prefeudal Saxon tribes prior to the Norman invasion.[20] It was seen as a golden age of English liberty free from the decadent influences of monarchical authority and feudal tenure. Specifically, this Ancient Constitution was supposed to have secured the freedom of individuals to participate in making governmental policies affecting their private property (notably taxation) and the freedom from governmental regulation of their private conduct in economic, political, social, and religious matters.[21] As such, the principles of this venerable constitution were decidedly hostile to monarchical feudalism, which regarded all landed property within the realm as possessed and granted by the sovereign and which conceived of those various spheres of life (economic, political, religious) which the Ancient Constitution regarded as "private" as integral parts of an organic whole, properly ordered under His Majesty.

---

[19] Wills, *Inventing America,* pp. 168–72, 237–39; J. G. A. Pocock, *The Machiavellian Moment* (Princeton, N.J.: Princeton University Press, 1969); Gordon Wood, *The Creation of the American Republic* (Chapel Hill: University of North Carolina Press, 1969).

[20] J. G. A. Pocock, *The Ancient Constitution and the Feudal Law* (Cambridge: Cambridge University Press, 1957); Bailyn, *Ideological Origins of the American Revolution,* pp. 80–82.

[21] Bailyn; ibid., Isaac Kramnick, "Republican Revisionism Revisited," *American Historical Review* 87 (June 1982): 629–64, at 638.

This vision of human psychology (as free and independent individuals) and politics (as a limited, consensual state) bore a rather striking resemblance to the Lockean liberal view of man and society, with one notable exception: these ideas, by deriving from an ancient source, provided historical validity to liberalism by existing prior to the feudal monarchy, which claimed political legitimacy through tradition and ancestral lineage. This notion of a prefeudal, Saxon constitution thus served the seventeenth-century parliamentarians, who invented it, by providing the essential substance of modern liberal doctrine with the advantage of beating the traditionalists at their own game by situating their historical claim to liberty in a period antedating the monarchy.

Thomas Jefferson inherited this concept of the Ancient Constitution from those English jurisprudence scholars who originally developed it. As a loyal British subject studying for the bar after the Glorious Revolution, he could not have avoided imbibing this common doctrine from the law books he was required to read. And while Jefferson referred to Sir Edward Coke as "an old dull scoundrel,"[22] his *Commonplace Book* of legal studies reveals ample use of Coke's version of English common law history. And from the archetypical liberal jurisprudence scholar Sir William Blackstone, Jefferson copied a classic description of the "corruption" of ancient Saxon liberties by the Norman conquerors who imposed feudalism on the island: "English liberties are not infringements merely of the king's prerogative, extorted from princes by taking advantage of their weakness; but a restoration of that ancient constitution, of which our ancestors had been defrauded by the art and finesse of the Norman Lawyers, rather than deprived by the force of Norman arms."[23] The "art and finesse" of parliamentary lawyers was more than sufficient to restore that Ancient Constitution in seventeenth-century England, and Jefferson, in his ideological battle with the British Empire, one hundred years later, was to take lessons from them.

Jefferson's journal of legal studies reveals more than a casual acquaintance with the classics in English common law history. Included are nearly all of the major works on the subject—

---

[22] Jefferson to John Page, December 25, 1762, *Papers*, 1: 5.
[23] Jefferson, *Commonplace Book*, entry 740.

traditional and modern. Significant extracts appear from Coke's *Institutes* (1671); Salked's *Reports of Cases in King's Bench, 1689–1712* (1717–18); Lord Kames's *Historical Law Tracts* (1758); Sir John Henry Dalrymple's *Essay towards a General History of Feudal Property* (1757); Sir Henry Spelman's *Glossarium Archaiologicum* (1664)—which historian J. G. A. Pocock considers the first complete and accurate account of English feudalism;[24] William Somner's *Treatise of Gavelkind* (1660); Sir William Blackstone's *Commentaries on the Laws of England* (1765–68); Francis Stoughton Sullivan's *Historical Treatise on the Feudal Law and the Constitution and Laws of England* (1772); and Dilly's *Historical Essay on the English Constitution . . . from the First Establishment of the Saxons in this Kingdom* (1771); along with references to the contemporaneous theorists Montesquieu, Hume, and Locke.[25]

In spite of this broad and balanced study of English constitutionalism, Jefferson, in his citing of these references in his revolutionary writings, shows a decidedly selective use of their arguments in favor of those acknowledging and endorsing the Ancient Constitution. That is, Jefferson follows his liberal parliamentarian predecessors in asserting the rights of this venerable Saxon constitution against the legitimacy of the Crown (and the empire). For example, when the work of traditionalist Sir John Dalrymple, which found English feudalism beginning in those Saxon tribes themselves (and only subsequently consolidated by William the Conqueror), is attacked by William Somner's *Treatise of Gavelkind* (arguing for the purity of Saxon liberty), Jefferson applauds the latter, declaring Somner "the better Saxon scholar."[26] He is somewhat harsher with Francis Stoughton Sullivan. After noting significant passages in Sullivan's *Historical Treatise on the Feudal Law and the Constitution and Laws of England* which deny the historical validity of the Ancient Constitution while endorsing royal feudalism, Jefferson comments, "he

---

[24] Pocock, *The Ancient Constitution*, p. 88.
[25] Jefferson, *Commonplace Book*, entries 30–577, 733–54, 767–803, 905–appendix.
[26] Ibid., entries 569–77, 738.

shews himself to have imbibed principles very unfriendly to the rights of mankind and favorable to the pretended divine rights of the King."[27] This comment is especially telling because it directly links the historical argument of the Ancient Constitution with abstract natural rights philosophy, for Sullivan's historical denial of Saxon liberty doesn't merely violate English antiquity, it is "unfriendly to the *rights of Man*" (emphasis added). Erosion of liberalism's historical argument also bolsters the king's claim in medieval natural law philosophy against the competing view of man and society found in Locke's natural rights philosophy. Jefferson's need to defend the historical validity of the Ancient Constitution with the suprahistorical natural rights of Locke's philosophy at once shows the tenuous nature of that historical argument and its complementary status with philosophical liberalism.

Still, one can hardly blame Jefferson for adopting this historical fiction: The majority of books published on the subject after 1660 supported the Ancient Constitution as reflected in those copied into Jefferson's legal journal.[28] The myth of prefeudal Saxon liberty was as much a part of the Anglo-American ethos as John Locke's *Second Treatise,* and, as we have seen, the two complemented each other very nicely.

The principles of the Ancient Constitution found their way into Jefferson's writings directly, as in his passing reference to English history in his *Summary View of the Rights of British America*:

> The introduction of Feudal tenures into the Kingdom of England, though antient, is well enough understood. . . . In the earlier ages of the Saxon settlement, feudal holdings were certainly altogether

---

[27]Ibid., note to entry 767, p. 244.

[28]Jefferson found plenty of support for the Ancient Constitution in Sir Edward Coke's *Institutes of the Laws of England* (1671); Salked's *Reports of Cases in King's Bench 1689–1712* (1717–18); Lord Kames's *Historical Law Tracts* (1758); Somner's *Treatise of Gavelkind* (1660); Blackstone's *Commentaries on the Laws of England* (1765–68); Robertson's *History of the Reign of the Emperor Charles V*; and Dilly's *Historical Essay on the English Constitution . . . from the First Establishment of the Saxons in this Kingdom* (1771) —all cited in Jefferson, *Commonplace Book.*

unknown. . . . Our Saxon ancestors held their lands, as they did their personal property, in absolute dominion. . . . William the Norman first introduced that system generally. . . . But still much was left in the hands of his Saxon subjects . . . not subject to feudal conditions.[29]

But more significantly, these ideas became transformed by Jefferson's colonial circumstances into a novel theory of empire, a theory leading directly to American independence.

In his *Declaration of the Causes and Necessity for Taking Up Arms* (1775), Jefferson gives the English one of his many history lessons on the settlement of America, which merges conveniently with the Ancient Constitution: "Our forefathers, inhabitants of the island of Britain, left their native land to seek on these shores a residence for civil & religious freedom. At the expense of their blood, to the ruin of their fortunes . . . they effected settlements in the inhospitable wilds of America."[30] A year earlier Jefferson had explained the connection between this American settlement and its Saxon precursor:

> Our ancestors, before their emigration to America, were the free inhabitants of the British dominions in Europe, and possessed a right, which nature has given to all men, of departing from the country in which chance, not choice has placed them. . . . their Saxon ancestors had under this universal law, in like manner, left their native wilds and woods in the North of Europe. . . . and there never was any claim of superiority or dependence asserted over them by that mother country from which they had migrated. . . . no circumstance has occurred to distinguish materially the British from the Saxon migration.[31]

Interestingly, the "universal law" of the "right of departure" which the ancient Saxons exercised is established in Locke's *Second Treatise*.[32] Elsewhere, Jefferson grounded colonial inde-

---

[29]Jefferson, *Papers*, 1: 132.

[30]Thomas Jefferson, *Declaration of the Causes and Necessity for Taking Up Arms*, ibid., 1: 199.

[31]Thomas Jefferson, *A Summary of the Rights of British America*, ibid., 1: 121–22.

[32]John Locke, *The Second Treatise of Government* in *Two Treatises of Government*, ed. Peter Laslett (New York: New American Library, 1965), 8: 121–22.

pendence in the "labor" expended acquiring the new territory, which also comes directly out of Locke.[33]

From Jefferson's rendition of American liberties and de facto independence, following the precedent of their Saxon ancestors (with only occasional intrusions from John Locke), came his original theory of the British Empire. In this theory, the empire was made up of a federation of independent and equal legislatures, colonial (the commonwealths of Virginia, Pennsylvania, etc.) and domestic (the Parliament). These free and independent states then chose a common king as an arbiter to protect the rights of each legislature from any threat from foreign nations or each other. As with the governmental arbiter created by the free and equal individuals out of Locke's state of nature, the British Crown, in Jefferson's view, exercised delegated authority and was strictly limited to protecting the rights of those independent and equal legislatures making up the empire.

It is as such that Jefferson addressed "his Majesty" as "the chief magistrate of the British empire" and expected him to redress the colonies' "injured rights" from "his imperial throne."[34] He reminded the monarch that a king "is no more than the chief officer of the people," appointed by the people to enhance the "great machine of government."[35] And America's participation in the royal empire is not a consequence of the extension of a medieval realm, as much as a blessing bestowed by magnanimous colonists on their unfortunate English brethren. As Jefferson calmly explained to George III: "That settlements having been thus effected in the wilds of America, the emigrants thought proper to adopt that system of laws under which they had hitherto lived in the Mother Country, and to continue their union with her by submitting themselves to the same common sovereign, who was thereby made the central link connecting the several parts of the empire thus newly multiplied."[36] Or, put slightly differently a year later: "To continue their connection with the friends whom they had left they arranged themselves

---

[33] Jefferson, *Papers,* 1: 122, 133; and Locke, ibid., 5: 27, 32–33.
[34] Jefferson, ibid., p. 121.
[35] Ibid.
[36] Ibid., 1: 122–23.

by charters of compact under the same common king, who thus completed their powers of full and perfect legislation and became the link of union between the several parts of the empire."[37] The problem arose, from Jefferson's perspective, when one free and independent legislature within the federated empire (the British Parliament) began legislating for other free and equal legislatures (the colonies) and the supposedly neutral arbiter collaborated with the usurpers.

So, Jefferson first directed his complaints to Parliament, for exercising sovereign authority beyond its legitimate purview, and second, to the king, for going along with, and even sanctioning, this usurpation of authority. He declared the imperial compact "invaded by the parliament" in a manner "dangerous to . . . the British empire."[38] The idea that "one *free and independent legislature* hereby takes upon itself to suspend the powers of another" (emphasis added) is patently absurd to Jefferson.[39] In the original British Empire, ruled by the absolute authority of a feudal monarch, the dissolution of inferior colonial legislatures would not appear the least bit absurd; but since that monarch had been supplanted by his own inferior legislature, Parliament, which now sought to rule the colonies as the king had, it made little sense. Such "unheard of . . . executive power," wrote Jefferson, constituted a "parliamentary tyranny."[40]

While Jefferson concentrated on this formal political corruption of the empire, he also complained of the substantive changes in imperial policy under the parliamentary tyranny. The mer-

---

[37] Jefferson, *Declaration of Causes and Necessity,* 1: 200. See also Jefferson's *Autobiography* (New York: Putnam, n.d.), pp. 31, 40.

[38] In Jefferson's draft of the *Declaration of Rights for Virginia* (1774), *Papers,* 1: 119.

[39] Jefferson, *A Summary View,* ibid., 1: 126. Compare Locke's comment in the *Second Treatise,* para. 157 and 158: "It often comes to pass that in government where part of the legislative consists of representatives chosen by the people that by tract of time this representation becomes very unequal and disproportionate to the reasons it was at first established. . . . For it being the interest as well as intention of the people to have a fair and equal representative, whoever brings it nearest to that is an undoubted friend to and establisher of the government and cannot miss the consent and approbation of the community" (cited in Kramnick, "Republican Revisionism Revisited," p. 638).

[40] Jefferson, ibid., pp. 124–26.

chants who controlled Parliament "indulged themselves in every exorbitance which their avarice could dictate."[41] For example, while the Crown had always regulated colonial trade, this Parliament was extending that regulation into areas heretofore held sacred. Particularly disturbing to Jefferson was the rendering of American lands or estates subject to creditors. This violated the traditional immunity that the landed nobility enjoyed against the "Shylocks" of trade and money-lending.[42] It threatened to place gentlemen at the mercy of their lessers, a fate not welcomed by the heavily indebted Virginia gentry.

But Jefferson only alluded to this concern, perhaps because too vigorous a defense of landed rights came dangerously close to endorsing feudal tenure, which contradicted his firm adherence to the virtues of the prefeudal Ancient Constitution. So he returned to his original objection, asserting that "the true ground on which we declare these acts void is that the British Parliament has no right to exercise authority over us."[43] Thus, Jefferson wrote to John Randolph of his sincere desire for reconciliation with a benevolent monarch (if only it would restrain the "inordinate desires of Parliament"), but insisted that "I am of those too who rather than submit to the right of legislating for us by the British Parliament . . . would lend my hand to sink the whole island in the ocean."[44]

Having patiently explained to the king of Great Britain "the whole art of government"[45] and the proper ordering of the British Empire, Jefferson was able to regard George III's contempt for

---

[41] Ibid., p. 124. J. G. A. Pocock uses this and other colonial references to "corruption" to support his contention that they responded by invoking a "quasi-republican alternative" (*Virtue, Commerce and History* [Cambridge: Cambridge University Press, 1985], pp. 77–83), and that Jefferson called on George III to be Bolingbroke's "Patriot King." Isaac Kramnick's *Bolingbroke and His Circle* (Cambridge, Mass.: Harvard University Press, 1968, pp. 4, 56, 61, 76–77, 82–83) seems to suggest that this classical republican interpretation confuses eighteenth-century Tory virtue (landed traditional hierarchy) with classical Greek virtue (participation) and both with the liberal Ancient Constitution.

[42] Jefferson, ibid., p. 124.

[43] Ibid., p. 125.

[44] Ibid., pp. 242, 129–30, 424–27.

[45] Ibid., p. 134.

his kind advice as an abdication of royal authority, effectively eliminating the duty of allegiance owed that sovereign. This must have provided some comfort to Jefferson, for, as he had learned in his legal studies: treason being a breach of allegiance to the king, "if there is no allegiance, there can be no treason."[46] The American colonies' assertion of independence was thus presented not as a breaking of legitimate ties to a traditional realm, but merely the reclaiming of their ancient liberties from an irresponsible and corrupt monarchy.

The problem with Jefferson's reliance on the Ancient Constitution as a basis for legitimizing American independence was the questionable historical validity of that Saxon precedent and the consequences of basing his arguments on historical inaccuracies. As historian J. G. A. Pocock has shown in his definitive work on the subject, this notion of an Ancient Constitution as "a golden age, a lost paradise in which Englishmen had enjoyed liberties that had been taken from them and must be restored" was invented during the seventeenth-century political struggles between the king and Parliament.[47] Specifically, parliamentarians wishing to ground their rights in some basis exclusive of royal prerogative and feudal privilege found an ideal place in a pre-feudal constitutional tradition antedating the Crown and preserved in the common law.[48] A hereditary monarchy which premised its legitimacy on generations of tradition could be dethroned with a constitution of even greater antiquity—or so reasoned the parliamentarians who invoked the rights of the Ancient Constitution. But as Pocock has shown, these "constitutionalists were forced into a kind of historical obscurantism—compelled to attribute their liberties to more and more remote and mythical periods in the effort to prove them independent of the will of the kings."[49]

Unfortunately, those theories of Jefferson's which relied on

---

[46] Quoted from William Salked's *Reports of Cases in King's Bench 1689–1712* and copied into Jefferson's *Commonplace Book,* entry 242.
[47] Pocock, *The Ancient Constitution,* p. 126
[48] Ibid., p. 16.
[49] Ibid., p. 17.

this mythical Ancient Constitution also suffered dangers of historical inaccuracy, which eventually undermined the consistency of some of his revolutionary arguments. For, if the liberal jurisprudence scholars from whom Jefferson so assiduously borrowed erroneously premised their assaults on the monarchy in the nonexistent liberties of a mythical Ancient Constitution, Jefferson's imperial theories beholden to those scholars would share the taint of their mistakes. In both cases, the major historical blind spot would be the *feudal* basis of social organization and the common law tradition. Sir Edward Coke, as Pocock shows, "had no conception that in the early common law he was dealing with the law of a society organized upon feudal principles."[50] As such, it was possible for Coke to simply re-interpret the English common law through strictures adopted from modern natural rights philosophy. But this could not validate—historically—the pre–Norman Saxon liberties with which the parliamentarian wished to out-precedent the monarchy. For, in fact, the common law tradition did not preserve ancient Saxon liberties which supported parliamentary supremacy; the common law tradition represented the well-developed feudal relations brought to the island by William the Conqueror: "The Common Law was above all a law regulating the tenure of land, and the rules of tenure it contained in fact presupposed the existence of those military and feudal tenures which had been imported by the Normans."[51]

To the extent native Saxons possessed any organized society and government, it was tribal and chieftain rather than the ideal liberal order of John Locke. A later critic of the mythical Ancient Constitution described the Saxons as a crowd of "rude, scarce humanized fighting beggars."[52]

By adopting the historical inaccuracies of the parliamentary lawyers, Jefferson simply transferred their tenets repudiating monarchical feudalism to the last remaining remnant of royal absolutism: the traditional ideology of the royal empire (which, while the English parliamentarians had abolished its power at

---

[50] Ibid., p. 45.
[51] Ibid., p. 64.
[52] In Kramnick, *Bolingbroke and His Circle,* pp. 130–31.

home, for purposes of colonial control, retained it abroad). While this may seem ironic, in the least, or even just deserts for the English parliamentarians—whose own fallacious arguments were now used against them—it rendered certain of Jefferson's revolutionary writings mildly embarrassing. For just as the parliamentarians attempted to write royal feudalism out of English common law history, Thomas Jefferson attempted to write the Crown out of American colonial history, with, at times, questionable results.

Jefferson's peculiar form of historical tunnel-vision occurs most evidently in his interpretation of the settlement of Virginia. In October of 1775, King George III, addressing Parliament on the subject of American colonial unrest, declared that those settlements had been "planted with great tenderness, encouraged with many commercial advantages, and protected and defended at much expense and treasure."[53]

In response to this royal assertion of English nurturance of the American colonies, Jefferson wrote a history of Virginia, ostensibly showing the absence of such support and proving the "self-reliance" of American settlers. In his *Refutation of the Argument that the Colonies Were Established at the Expense of the British Nation* (January 1776),[54] Jefferson presented a detailed history of Virginia's settlement, from which any impartial examination would provide ample evidence not only for the king's assertions of British support, but for the feudal origins of that support. Yet Jefferson chose to conclude from this same evidence that American colonists were themselves solely responsible for their own settlement; and this historical blindspot may be attributed directly to his adherence to the doctrine of the Ancient Constitution (and its ignorance of the cultural basis of feudal tenure).

From a perspective such as Pocock's, acknowledging England's feudal past and recognizing its continued existence in the Elizabethan period during which Virginia was originally settled, the historical instances cited by Jefferson lead directly to the tradi-

---

[53] *Parliamentary History,* 18: 696, reprinted in Jefferson, *Papers,* 1: 277.

[54] Thomas Jefferson, *Refutation of the Argument that the Colonies Were Established at the Expense of the British Nation,* ibid., pp. 277–84.

tional conclusions he rejects. For example, he writes that in 1578 Queen Elizabeth granted, by letters of patent to Sir Humphrey Gilbert, a license to search for uninhabited countries, reserving for the Crown of England his allegiance.[55] That allegiance effectively transferred his discoveries to the Crown—to then be returned to him under the principle of feudal tenure. Elizabeth similarly granted support to Sir Walter Raleigh, with which he declared Newfoundland "in behalf of the Crown of England," afterwards ordaining that the laws of the realm include conformity in religion to the Church of England, and punishment for treason against the Crown (even against disrespectfully speaking of Her Majesty).[56] Raleigh proceeded to parcel out, in the form of feudal vassalage, portions of land to the fishermen by surrounding waters for their use in drying and dressing their fish, in exchange for a yearly rent to him and his heirs![57] One can hardly imagine a more self-conscious reenactment of feudal procedures and duties. In like manner, Raleigh settled Virginia, from which Jefferson concluded that "Raleigh, having received no assistance from the Crown in any of these enterprises and having now expended 40,000 pounds in them, made an assignment to divers gentlemen and merchants of London for continuing the action of inhabiting and planting his people in Virginia."[58] Ironically, Jefferson's "Refutation" ends with his observation that subsequent Virginia settlements were sanctioned by King James's 1624 Proclamation.[59]

Later in life, Jefferson acknowledged "some uncertainties and inaccuracies of historical facts" connected with his appropriation of the Ancient Constitution in his theory of empire and colonial history.[60] But in the heat of revolutionary turmoil, Jefferson

---

[55] Ibid., p. 277.
[56] Ibid., p. 278.
[57] Ibid.
[58] Ibid., p. 283.
[59] Ibid. And to George III's assertions premised in that proclamation Jefferson responded that "a King who can adopt falsehood, and solemnize it from the throne, justifies the revolution of fortune which reduces him to a private station" (ibid.).
[60] This was in 1809 in reference to Jefferson's *A Summary View, Papers,* 1: 670 (appendix).

refused to admit any errors in his approach, even when confronted with alternative evidence by trusted fellow revolutionaries.

In August of 1776, fellow-Virginian Edmund Pendleton wrote to Jefferson concerning the matter of land distribution in that newly-independent state and pointed out the feudal basis of land tenure under the Crown Empire, suggesting that it be retained in modified form: "The Charter on which the Colony was founded, intitled every Britain to settle to 50 acres of Land, to be held in Soccage by the Payments of an Annual quitrent. . . . It upon the whole therefore appears to me best to continue the old mode, transferring rights, former and future quitrents and Escheats to the Common Wealth from the Crown."[61] Jefferson's response to Pendleton's proposal reveals much greater concern over the latter's raising of legitimate feudal tenure as Virginia's base of land ownership than the practical issue of future regulation of land distribution and state revenue acquisition, a response that startled Pendleton (who did not realize the revolutionary implications of admitting the feudal origins of America's public and private land).[62] Jefferson said: "The opinion that our lands were allodial possessions [i.e., grants free from feudal tenure obligations] is one which I have very long held, and had in my eye during a pretty considerable part of my law reading which I found always strengthened it."[63]

As we know now, Jefferson's law readings did not always support his belief in the Ancient Constitution; but, after admitting the possibility of its invalidity, Jefferson simply resorted to political expediency, declaring the issue "a mere speculative point" and urging unwavering adherence to "ancient virtues" in spite of their problematical validity:

> But this is only meant with respect to the English law as transplanted here [i.e. the Ancient Constitution]. How far our acts of

---

[61] Ibid., pp. 484–85. This also shows that Louis Hartz was incorrect in asserting in *The Liberal Tradition in America* (New York: Harcourt Brace, 1955) that America has no feudal past; we had it (albeit in corrupted form) in the organic ideology of the early British Empire.

[62] Edmund Pendleton to Thomas Jefferson, August 26, 1776, *Papers,* 1: 507.

[63] Ibid., p. 491.

assembly or acceptance of grants may have converted lands which were allodial into feuds [i.e. from lands independent of royal authority into lands possessed under the crown's feudal tenure] I have never considered. This matter is now a mere speculative point; and we have it in our power to make it what it ought to be for the public good.[64]

This uncharacteristic rejection of historical reasoning supportive of revolutionary right and acceptance of an essentially "might makes right" argument is quickly followed by Jefferson's general denunciation of the monarchical feudal system, in an attempt to justify his revolutionary position in spite of its tenuousness: "Is not its history well known, and the purposes for which it was introduced, to wit, the establishment of a military system of defense? Was it not afterwards made an engine of immense oppression? Is it wanting with us for the purpose of military defense? May not its other legal effects . . . be performed in other more simple ways?"[65] This elaborate interrogatory constituting a rejection of feudalism on pragmatic terms, Jefferson now returned to his praise of "antient Saxon laws," notwithstanding their invalidation by the acknowledgement of the actual feudal grounding which superseded them. "Are we not the better for what we have hitherto abolished of the feudal system? Has not every restitution of the antient Saxon laws had happy effects? Is it not better now that we return at once to that happy system of our ancestors, the wisest and most perfect ever yet devised by the wit of man, as it stood before the 8th century?"[66]

Given Pendleton's mild inquisition, Jefferson's spirited response seems to "protest too much," indicating some realization on his part that his revolutionary rationalizations were getting into deep water. But, in a sense, of course, Jefferson was correct in determining the issue of feudal tenure to be irrelevant, though not for the reasons of revolutionary expediency or "antient virtue" he invoked. Rather, his historical inaccuracies were rendered somewhat irrelevant by their status as errors perpetrated on a fraud—namely the continued existence of the organic (feudal)

---

[64] Ibid.
[65] Ibid., p. 492.
[66] Ibid.

ideology of the British Empire after Parliament had wrested sovereignty from the monarchy. The British could not have it both ways: either they could truly retain the organic realm with a legitimate feudal monarch at its head and reasonably expect colonial obedience to its extended form in the organic empire (but necessarily accept the same limitations imposed on the Americans, forfeiting parliamentary and mercantile supremacy) or they could admit that Parliament—with its commercial interests—had triumphed over the throne and feudalism, permanently altering the British Empire, as the English realm, and reconstruct imperial relations accordingly; but they could not expect to do away with the traditional realm at home and continue it abroad, retaining the royal trappings while infusing them with modern substance, particularly when the liberal ideals embodied in the Ancient Constitution and codified in modern law books (quickly acquired by American lawyers) enshrined freedom and equality.

On the other hand, Jefferson's expectations and demands, premised in the same mythical Ancient Constitution, were only slightly less unreasonable. He wanted de facto colonial independence (free from the historical obligations of an organic monarchical empire) premised in an imperial federation based on the Ancient Constitution, but he also expected the king to exercise impartial rule over the Parliament which had invented the Ancient Constitution and which had so recently chased his predecessor out of England. The source of these troubling contradictions resides in the historical confusions inherent in the Ancient Constitution itself, and may explain why Jefferson's most famous revolutionary document, the Declaration of Independence, relies almost exclusively on another, more abstract, theoretical justification for colonial revolution: John Locke's natural rights philosophy.

CHAPTER 3

REVOLUTIONARY AMERICA:
JEFFERSON'S LOCKEAN
INDEPENDENCE

IT IS interesting that Thomas Jefferson's most famous revolutionary document relies almost not at all on the elusive historical precedent of the Ancient Constitution and almost exclusively on the abstract natural rights philosophy of Lockean liberalism. This is exactly what the seventeenth-century English parliamentarians did, one hundred years earlier, as they increasingly shied away from the tenuous historical validity of the Ancient Constitution, preferring to conduct their ideological battles with the Crown on "self-evident" Lockean principles, whose abstractions eluded rigorous historical scrutiny. Still, Jefferson's use of natural rights philosophy in the Declaration of Independence was dramatically shaped by his conception of the British Empire, itself beholden to the Ancient Constitution. John Locke's notion of "free, equal, and independent" individuals takes on a rather different significance within Jefferson's view of a federated empire under an arbiter-king. And Jefferson's peculiar adaptation of Lockean categories raises questions concerning the quality of the influence of natural rights philosophy on Jefferson's own political thought, especially after the Revolution.

However, before examining the peculiar use to which Jefferson put Locke's theory, it is necessary to show conclusively that the

Declaration of Independence was, in fact, substantially influenced by John Locke's *Second Treatise,* as this elemental truth has lately been called into question.[1]

John Locke in Jefferson's Declaration of Independence

Perhaps the best way to show the incontrovertible presence of Locke's political theory in Jefferson's Declaration of Independence is through a thematic collation of the major theoretical concepts in each text. Three categories represent the major themes of Locke's political philosophy: (1) the nature of man, (2) the nature of government, and (3) the right of revolution. These categories also represent the order in which Locke presented his political philosophy, and the fact that Jefferson's text even follows this sequence further suggests the thematic influence. This method of comparing the texts of Locke and Jefferson seems more useful than the common analytic method of trying to match word for word and phrase for phrase, since the latter often misses the thematic forest for the verbal trees. Several striking verbal parallels do exist between Locke's *Second Treatise* and Jefferson's Declaration of Independence, but the substantive thematic parallels are of much greater significance. Simply put, they consist of the following:

1. *The nature of man*: Locke conceives of human nature as involving men who are naturally free, equal, and independent individuals possessed of natural rights, especially

---

[1] See Garry Wills, *Inventing America: Jefferson's* Declaration of Independence (New York: Doubleday, 1978), pp. 168–72. Evidently, Mr. Wills also missed Jefferson's reference to Locke's *Second Treatise* in his *The Commonplace Book of Thomas Jefferson: A Repertory of His Ideas on Government,* ed. Gilbert Chinard (Baltimore: Johns Hopkins Press, 1926), p. 214; and the letter of August 1771 (shortly after his first library burned) referring to "Locke on government—8vo" in Jefferson's *The Papers of Thomas Jefferson,* 20 vols., ed. Julian Boyd (Princeton, N.J.: Princeton University Press, 1950), 1: 77–79. Also see Steven Dworetz, *The Unvarnished Doctrine: Locke, Liberalism and the American Revolution* (Durham, N.C.: Duke University Press, 1990).

that of continued physical existence (self-preservation), and of qualities necessarily attending that existence (liberty and property).

2. *The nature of government*: Following from his notion of human nature, Locke's conception of legitimate government consists in that impartial, disinterested arbiter established by those free, equal, and independent individuals possessed of natural rights who by their consent submit to the authority of government constructed to secure their natural rights from the violation of other individuals.

3. *The right of revolution*: The natural right to abolish established governments follows from the first two Lockean conceptions, or rather, from their disjuncture. That is, given Locke's definition of human nature and legitimate government, it follows that if the established institutions of government ever fail to secure the rights they were created to guarantee (and even establish a tyranny—invading those rights themselves), it is appropriate for the people to abolish that political structure and erect one that will correctly perform its legitimate function (which is limited to securing individual rights).

Now let us review the relevant portion of Jefferson's text in its entirety:[2]

When in the course of human events it becomes necessary for a people to advance from that subordination in which they have hitherto remained, & to assume among the powers of the earth the equal & independent station to which the laws of nature & of nature's god entitle them, a decent respect to the opinions of mankind requires that they should declare the causes which impel them to change.

We hold these truths to be sacred & undeniable; that all men are created equal & independent, that from that equal creation they derive rights inherent and inalienable, among which are the preservation of life, & liberty, & the pursuit of happiness;[3] and to

---

[2]This is Jefferson's "original Rough Draught," i.e., his fair copy as prepared for the Committee and prior to Congress's revisions, in *Papers*, 1: 423–27.

[3]Much has been written on Jefferson's substitution of "happiness" for Locke's

secure these ends, governments are instituted among men, deriving their just powers from the consent of the governed; that whenever any form of government shall become destructive of these ends, it is the right of the people to alter or to abolish it & to institute new government, laying its foundation on such principles & organizing its powers in such form, as to them shall seem most likely to effect their safety & happiness. Prudence indeed will dictate that governments long established should not be changed for light & transient causes: and accordingly all experience hath shewn that mankind are more disposed to suffer while evils are sufferable than to right themselves by abolishing the forms to which they are accustomed. But when a long train of abuses & usurpations, begun

---

"Property" or "Estate." Liberal Jeffersonians Gilbert Chinard, Joyce Appleby, and John Diggins see this as coming from other revolutionary pamphlets and Lockean ideals—that freedom, property, and equal opportunity produce human happiness: Gilbert Chinard, *Thomas Jefferson: The Apostle of Americanism* (Boston: Little, Brown, 1929), p. 73; Joyce Appleby, "What Is Still American in the Political Philosophy of Thomas Jefferson," *William and Mary Quarterly* 39 (April 1982): 287–309, at 287; John Diggins, *The Lost Soul of American Politics* (New York: Basic Books, 1984), p. 37. My interpretation tends to be more congenial with Forrest McDonald's claim in *Novus Ordo Seclorum: The Intellectual Origins of the Constitution* (Lawrence: University Press of Kansas, 1985; pp. ix–x) that Jefferson's interest in happiness derives from Aristotle, as it is the subject of book 1 of his *Nicomachean Ethics*. Aristotle writes, "since all knowledge and every choice is directed toward some good, let us discuss what is in our view the aim of politics, i.e., the highest good attainable by action. As far as its name is concerned, most people would probably agree: for both the common run of people and cultivated men call it happiness" (section 4, p. 6).

Happiness is also related to politics, especially the politics of the Greek polis, by Baron De Montesquieu, when he writes, "in every [Greek] republic the legislator had in view the happiness of the citizens . . . with the enjoyment of a small territory and great happiness, it was easy for the number of the citizens to increase" (*The Spirit of the Laws*, 2 vols., trans. Thomas Nugent [New York: Hafner, 1975] 2: 10).

Jefferson's appreciation of the public and private dimensions of happiness are revealed in his advice given to nephew Peter Carr (1788): "Be assiduous in learning, take much exercise for your health, and practice much virtue. Health, learning and virtue will insure your happiness; they will give you a quiet conscience, private esteem and public honor" (*The Writings of Thomas Jefferson*, ed. A. E. Bergh, "Memorial Edition" [Washington, D.C.: Thomas Jefferson Memorial Assoc., 1904–05] 2: 409). His application of the principle to government is revealed in a letter to M. VanDerKemp (1812): "The only orthodox object of the institution of government is to secure the greatest degree of happiness possible to the general mass of those associated under it" (ibid., 6: 45).

at a distinguished period, & pursued invariably the same object, evinces a design to subject them to arbitrary power, it is their right, it is their duty, to throw off such government & to provide new guards for their future security. Such has been the patient sufferance of these colonies; & such is now the necessity which constrains them to expunge their former systems of government. The history of his present majesty, is a history of unremitting injuries and usurpations . . . all of which have in direct object the establishment of an absolute tyranny . . . let facts be submitted . . .

The thematic collation in tables 1, 2, and 3 not only reveals the incontestable theoretical influence of Locke's *Second Treatise* on Jefferson's Declaration of Independence, but also shows that Thomas Jefferson provided perhaps the clearest and most concise presentation of John Locke's political theory ever distilled from Locke's *Second Treatise of Government*.[4]

JEFFERSON'S MODIFICATION OF LOCKEAN LIBERALISM

The connection between Locke's ideas and Jefferson's Declaration of Independence is quite clear; what remains to be shown is the alteration of those liberal ideals by Jefferson's peculiar colonial circumstances.

The "facts submitted" to prove George III's arbitrary power are less interesting than that they were addressed to the king. Their content is thus only understood in light of Jefferson's theory of empire; that is, a voluntary federation of "equal and independent" states overseen by an impartial monarch securing the rights of each. The primary right to be secured is the fundamental quality of political existence: local, autonomous control of legislation. It is this essential right of democratic sovereignty that these enumerated complaints entail:

1. The king "has refused his assent to laws the most wholesome and necessary for the public good";

---

[4]The phrases of John Locke's are extracted from the best edition available of his *Second Treatise of Government,* in *Two Treatises of Government,* ed. Peter Laslett (New York: New American Library, 1965).

TABLE 1. THE NATURE OF MAN

Jefferson's Declaration of Independence	Locke's *Second Treatise of Government*
"We hold these truths to be sacred & undeniable; that all men are created equal and independent"*	"Mankind . . . being all equal and independent"* (ch. 2, p. 6) "all men by nature are equal" (ch. 4, p. 54) "Men being, as has been said, by Nature, all free, equal and independent" (ch. 8, p. 95)
"from that equal creation they derive rights inherent and inalienable"	"that equal Right that every man hath, to his Natural Freedom" (ch. 6, p. 54)
"among which are the preservation* of life, & liberty,* & the pursuit of happiness"	"Man being born, as has been proved, with a Title to perfect Freedom, and an uncontroled enjoyment of all the Rights and Privileges of the Law of Nature, equally with any other Man, or number of men in the world, hath by Nature a Power, not only to preserve his Property, that is, his Life, Liberty* and Estate, against the Injuries and Attempts of other Men; but to judge of, and punish the breaches of that Law in others" (ch. 7, p. 87) "Everyone as he is bound to preserve* himself" (ch. 2, p. 6) "Men, being once born, have a right to their preservation"* (ch. 5, p. 25)

*Indicates verbal parallels between Declaration of Independence and *Second Treatise*.

TABLE 2. THE NATURE OF GOVERNMENT

Jefferson's Declaration of Independence	Locke's *Second Treatise of Government*
"to secure these ends, governments are instituted . . . deriving their just powers from the consent* of the governed"	"Man . . . seeks . . . to joyn in society with others . . . to unite for the mutual Preservation of their Lives, Liberties and Estates" (ch. 9, p. 123)
	"Civil Society is . . . agreeing with other Men to joyn and unite . . . in a secure Enjoyment of their Properties, and a Greater Security"* (ch. 8, p. 95)
"to provide new guards for their future security"*	"And thus that, which begins and actually constitutes any Political Society, is nothing but the consent* . . . of a majority to unite and incorporate into such a society. And this is that, and that only, which did, or could give beginning to lawful Government in the World" (ch. 8, p. 99)
	"No one can be put out of his Estate, and subjected to the Political Power of another, without his own Consent"* (ch. 8, p. 95)
	"The Liberty of Man, in Society, is to be under no other Legislative Power, but that established, by consent"* (ch. 4, p. 22)
	"Political Power is that Power which every man having in the state of Nature, has given up into the hands of Society, and therein to the Governours. . . . That it shall be imployed for their good, and the preservation of their Property . . . their Lives, Liberties, and Possessions . . . only from Compact and Agreement, and the mutual Consent* of those who make up the Community" (ch. 15, p. 171)

*Indicates verbal parallels between Declaration of Independence and *Second Treatise*.

TABLE 3. THE RIGHT OF REVOLUTION

Jefferson's Declaration of Independence	Locke's *Second Treatise of Government*
"whenever any form of government shall become destructive of these ends, it is the right of the people to alter or abolish it & to institute new government"	"When by the Arbitrary Power . . . without the Consent and contrary to the common Interest of the People, there also the Legislative is altered" (ch. 19, p. 216)
	"when the Government is dissolved, the People are at Liberty to provide for themselves, by erecting a new Legislative" (ch. 19, p. 220)
"prudence indeed will dictate that governments long established should not be changed for light & transient cause"	"Revolutions happen not upon every little mismanagement in public affairs. Great mistakes in the ruling part, many wrong and inconvenient Laws, and all the slips of humans frailty will be born by the people, without mutiny or murmur" (ch. 19, p. 225)
"mankind are more disposed to suffer while evils are sufferable* than to right themselves* by abolishing the forms to which they are accustomed"*	"the People, who are more disposed to suffer,* than right themselves* by Resistence"* (ch. 19, p. 230)
"but when a long train of abuses* & usurpations . . . pursued invariably the same object,* evinces a design* to subject them to arbitrary power"*	"But if a long train of Abuses* . . . all tending the same way, make the design* visible to the People" (ch. 19, p. 225) "Absolute, Arbitrary Power"* (ch. 4, p. 23)
"it is their right, it is their duty, to throw off such government & to provide new guards for their future security"	" 'tis not to be wonder'd, that they should then rouze themselves, and endeavor to put the rule into such hands, which may secure to them the ends for which Government was at first erected" (ch. 19, p. 225)

*Indicates verbal parallels between Declaration of Independence and *Second Treatise.*

2. "he has forbidden his governors to pass laws";
3. "he has refused to pass other laws . . . unless those people would relinquish the right of representation";
4. "he has dissolved Representative houses";
5. "he has refused . . . others to be elected";
6. he has prevented immigration to colonies and new land appropriations;
7. he has refused to assent to laws establishing judiciary powers;
8. he has made judges dependent on his will;
9. he has erected multitudinous new offices;
10. he has kept standing armies in times of peace;
11. he has rendered the military above the civilian authority;
12. he has subjected us to "a jurisdiction foreign to our constitutions" (i.e., Parliament);
13. he has protected usurpers with mock trials;
14. he has cut off colonial trade with the world;
15. he has "imposed taxes on us without our consent";
16. he has deprived us of "trial by jury";
17. he has transported defendants across the sea;
18. he is "taking away our charters & altering fundamentally the forms of our governments";
19. by "suspending our own legislatures."

As such, King George III had violated the rights of the American colonies, and thereby abdicated government "declaring us out of his allegiance & protection."[5] This, then, allowed the colonies to "reject and renounce all allegiance & subjection to the kings of Great Britain . . . [as] we utterly dissolve and break off all political connection which may have heretofore subsisted between us & the people or parliament of Great Britain . . . and declare these colonies to be free and independent states."[6]

It may thus be seen that Jefferson has adapted the language of Lockean liberalism, created originally for individual men in

---

[5]Jefferson, *Papers,* 1: 425. The remaining complaints concern Britain's resorting to violence to impose its will on America. Reference is made to the real or threatened use of foreign mercenaries, Indian savages, American loyalists, and insurgent slaves for this purpose, pp. 425–26.

[6]Ibid., p. 427.

the state of nature, to the needs of revolutionary colonies in a federated empire of equal and independent states. He therefore refers to "a people['s]" necessity to assume "equal and independent" status, meaning American legislatures[7] attaining proper equality with the British legislature. Locke's "free and independent" individuals are translated into Jefferson's "free and independent states,"[8] revealing the creative adaptation of Locke's theories to the needs of revolutionary colonies; but not necessarily indicating complete agreement with the Lockean content of those individual legislatures, or, as we shall see, (in chapter 4 below), Jefferson's undeviating adherence to Lockean conceptions of human nature and politics as absolute principles. In fact, Jefferson's mature political theory shifts markedly from the Lockean notions toward more classical conceptions of the psyche and the polis; and these postrevolutionary ideas cannot be reconciled with Jefferson's writings unless the context of his appeal to Locke in the Declaration of Independence is properly understood.

Scholars have viewed the connection between John Locke and Thomas Jefferson in two ways. Traditional Jefferson scholars, adhering to the Lockean orthodoxy (Becker, Boyd, Malone, Chinard, Commager)[9] have acknowledged the connection and concluded that it renders all of Jefferson's political philosophy consistently Lockean. The liberal conceptions of human nature and government found in Jefferson's revolutionary writings simply continue into his postrevolutionary thought, and our "Jeffersonian" tradition in America is a Lockean tradition of individual rights and limited government.

---

[7] Or, as Jefferson writes elsewhere, "these colonies," ibid., p. 424.

[8] Ibid., p. 427. Further evidence for this view of Jefferson's adaption of Lockean principles to revolutionary purposes appears in an early letter referring to the "independent rights" of "our . . . country"; see Jefferson to Archibald Cary and Benjamin Harrison, December 9, 1774, ibid., p. 154.

[9] Carl Becker, *The Declaration of Independence: A Study in the History of Political Ideas* (New York: Random House, 1958); Chinard, *Thomas Jefferson;* Julian P. Boyd, *The Declaration of Independence: The Evolution of the Text* (Princeton, N.J.: Princeton University Press, 1945); Henry Steele Commager, "The Declaration of Independence," in *Thomas Jefferson: The Man . . . His World . . . His Influence,* ed. Lally Weymouth (New York: Putnam, 1973); Dumas Malone, *Jefferson And His Time: Jefferson the Virginian,* vol. 1 (Boston: Little, Brown, 1948), ch. 16.

The revisionist scholars that challenge the Lockean orthodoxy in early American historiography also charge that Jefferson's Declaration of Independence was not Lockean in character. J. G. A. Pocock argues that the Declaration reflects "quasi-republican" ideology emphasizing a social human nature and Aristotelean public virtue.[10] Garry Wills claims that Jefferson's Declaration grows out of his adherence to Scottish moral sense philosophy, positing a naturally social human nature based in sympathy and benevolence.[11]

Both of these views of Jefferson's relation to Locke are partially correct, but incomplete. The traditional Jeffersonians are right about Locke's influence on the Declaration of Independence, but because they misunderstand the revolutionary character of that document, incorrectly project the continuing presence of Lockean liberalism on Jefferson's postrevolutionary thought. In fact, as we shall see, following the Revolution Jefferson's political ideas, preoccupied with the construction of a new republic, moved closer to classical categories, reserving his Lockean tendencies for occasional attacks on the national (federal) government (which by virtue of its distance from local democracy, its domination by "corrupt" commercial policies led by Hamilton's Federalists, and its proper purview in foreign affairs, constituted a menace to independent legislatures not unlike the king's Parliament). The revisionist Jeffersonians are correct in identifying another influence on Jefferson, and even in identifying it with the moral sense psychology and Aristotelean politics, but mistakenly project that later influence onto the earlier Declaration of Independence, which, as has been shown, *was* Lockean; though it may be argued that even in this instance, when Jefferson is clearly Lockean vis-à-vis remote corrupt government, he is already republican with respect to local legislative politics.

A proper understanding of Thomas Jefferson's Declaration of Independence, within the context of his entire political theory, admits the clear, if altered, influence of Locke's *Second Treatise of Government* on the text of that colonial revolutionary docu-

---

[10]J. G. A. Pocock, *Virtue, Commerce, and History* (Cambridge: Cambridge University Press, 1985), pp. 77–84.

[11]Wills, *Inventing America.*

ment. As such, it proscribes the promiscuous application of that influence on Jefferson's postrevolutionary theories, where, unbothered by the excesses of a corrupted Royal Empire and the whimsies of the Ancient Constitution, Jefferson could invest them with the richness of classical political thought. Still, Jefferson's development of classical republican theory in America does not entirely exclude Lockean liberalism, as he sees active, qualified citizens as the best preservers of individual natural rights.

CHAPTER 4

AMERICA AS A NEW REPUBLIC:
JEFFERSON'S CLASSICAL
DEMOCRACY

WHEN JEFFERSON returned to Virginia from Philadelphia in 1776, he immediately began effecting the reforms that would develop into his mature political philosophy. Having severed ties with the British Empire with ideas drawn from Lockean liberalism, Jefferson began constructing a new republic through classical republican ideas drawn from Aristotle, Montesquieu, Harrington, and the nonliberal Scottish moral sense philosophers. Jefferson saw the struggle for independence as a means to the more important end of establishing a virtuous republic in America. As he wrote in a letter of the time: "It is work of the most interesting nature. . . . In truth it is the whole object of the present controversy; for should a bad government be instituted for us, in future it had been as well to have accepted at first the bad one offered us from beyond the water without the risk and expense of contest."[1] This period of Jefferson's life, when he was reforming the laws of Virginia, provided the leisure with which he could begin formulating his mature political philosophy. Soon

---

[1] Jefferson to Thomas Nelson, Jr., May 16, 1776, *The Writings of Thomas Jefferson*, 10 vols., ed. Paul L. Ford (New York, 1897), 2:1–2.

to be drawn into active political life, filled with crises and expediency, Jefferson would not enjoy such luxury of philosophical
leisure until his retirement from the presidency, when many of
these early themes of classical politics were further developed.[2]

Jefferson's essential political philosophy may be understood
by examining his conceptions of human nature and political
society, and the complementary notions of economics, education,
and leadership and representation. Within this theoretical frame-
work, Jefferson's central political thought is closer to classical
republicanism than to Lockean liberalism by virtue of (1) his
conception of human nature as essentially social, inherently destined for life in community and requiring political society to
cultivate and develop man's innate social nature; (2) his vision
of the polity as deliberatively nurturing citizens' social faculties,
through direct participation in community life and governance,
and providing the economic, educational, and political prerequi-

---

[2]In several ways, the years immediately following Jefferson's writing of the
Declaration of Independence and those following his retirement from the presidency were much alike: both involved periods of removal from direct participation in politics but were distinguished by intense intellectual activity; and each
evidenced the clearest description of his mature theory, delineated around local
ward democracy and the educational, political, and economic policies implied
in that democracy. For Jefferson's own references connecting these two periods,
see his *Autobiography* (N.Y.: Putnam, n.d.), pp. 50–63; his letters to Monsieur
Coray, October 31, 1823, in *WTJ*, 20 vols., ed. Albert Ellery Bergh (Washington,
D.C.: Thomas Jefferson Memorial Assoc., 1904–05), 15:480–90; to Joseph C.
Cabell, January 31, 1814, *WTJ*, 14:84; and to John Adams, Oct. 28, 1813, in
The Adams-Jefferson Letters, 2 vols., ed. Lester J. Cappon (Chapel Hill: University
of North Carolina Press, 1959), 2: 387–92. Hannah Arendt's otherwise excellent
book *On Revolution* (New York: Viking, 1965) unfortunately attributes Jefferson's mature political theory (in ward democracy) exclusively to his later writings,
missing its origin in those early Virginia reforms and improperly characterizing
them as merely a continuation of his "revolutionary" spirit begun in the Declaration (Arendt, ibid, pp. 253–54) — thereby failing to distinguish between the
"destructive" purposes of that revolutionary document, premised in Lockean
liberalism, and the "constructive" purposes of his subsequent ideas, drawn from
classical categories. The absence of these ideas (of political participation, civic
education, economic independence, etc.) in Jefferson's policies while serving in
national political office (as vice president and president) may, as Henry Adams
asserted, show them as something of a pose. It may, however, indicate Jefferson's
depreciation of the importance of the federal government on domestic policies,
as suggested by his conception of federalism.

sites of that independent democratic citizenry; and (3) his conception of ethics, emphasizing the values of social cooperation and harmony most conducive to democratic self-governance. This view of Jefferson's political philosophy shows a rich constellation of moral sense psychology that recognizes man's social nature in feelings of sympathy and benevolence, classical politics requiring citizen participation, public education and economic independence linked to more centralized republics through a "natural aristocracy," and those elements of modern economics contributing to American virtue and self-sufficiency. Still, Jefferson's concern for individual rights and liberties did not disappear in this republican philosophy, as it is clear that he perceived participatory democracy as the best security against tyrannical government, and the protection of individual rights.

HUMAN NATURE — SOCIAL MAN

In contrast with Lockean liberalism, which conceived of man's nature as separate, isolated, and independent, Jefferson conceived of man as naturally social and political. He copied this quote from Lord Kames into his *Commonplace Book*: "Man, by his nature is fitted for society, and society, by its conveniences is fitted for man."[3] Jefferson attributed man's social nature to an innate "moral sense." The individual's moral sense, which renders society his natural home, consisted, for Jefferson, of three distinct but interrelated qualities: (1) the human capacity for moral choice, or the knowledge of good and evil and the freedom to

---

[3]Thomas Jefferson, *The Commonplace Book of Thomas Jefferson: A Repertory of His Ideas on Government*, ed. Gilbert Chinard, (Baltimore: Johns Hopkins Press, 1926), p. 107. Cf. Bolingbroke's remark that God made man "by nature fit for society" (quoted in Isaac Kramnick, *Bolingbroke and His Circle*, [Cambridge, Mass.: Harvard University Press, 1968], p. 89). Cf. Aristotle, in *The Politics,* "man is by nature a political animal," trans. T. A. Sinclair (Baltimore: Penguin, 1972), book 1, ch. 2, p. 28.

Richard Matthews, in *The Radical Politics of Thomas Jefferson* (Lawrence: University Press of Kansas, 1984), p. 53, reaches essentially the same conclusion through another means: examining Jefferson's writings on blacks and Indians and deducing a theory of human nature.

act on that knowledge in choosing the good;[4] (2) an innate identification with others, a feeling of sympathy for others' concerns and sufferings, and a pleasure in the relief of others' pain and their attaining happiness;[5] (3) from the combination of these two qualities, a natural sense of justice, making social life possible and beneficial, as this appreciation for justice allows the individual to feel concern for the good of others and for the whole community of which he is a part. This inherent sense of justice remained for Jefferson "the first excellence of a well-ordered" society and a necessary ingredient for individual happiness.[6] Hence, Jefferson encouraged his young ward Peter Carr to be "good, learned and industrious," insisting that such virtues would make him "precious to your country, dear to your friends, happy within yourself."[7]

Adhering to this social vision of human nature, Jefferson became increasingly critical of the modern liberal psychology which conceived of man as naturally individualistic, and of its corollary view of the state as merely a conventional artifice or "social contract" limited to preserving private rights of self-interest and self-preservation. Jefferson insisted that liberal natural law phi-

---

[4]Jefferson to Peter Carr, August 10, 1787, *WTJ*, 6:257; to John Adams, February 25, 1823, *A-JL*, 2:589. Cf. Aristotle, "the real differences between man and other animals is that humans alone have perception of good and evil, right and wrong, just and unjust" (*Politics*, book 1, ch. 2, p. 29); and "for man's moral choice to be completely excellent, he must know what he is doing; secondly, he must choose to act the way he does, and choose it for its own sake; and in the third place, the act must spring from a firm and unchangeable character" (*Nicomachean Ethics*, trans. Martin Ostwald [Indianapolis: Bobbs-Merrill, 1962], book 2, 1105a, p. 39; cf. *Genesis* 2:15; 3:5).

[5]Jefferson to Thomas Law, June 13, 1814, *The Complete Jefferson*, ed. Saul K. Padover (New York: Tudor, 1943), p. 1033; to John Adams, October 14, 1816, *A-JL*, 2:492. Cf. Rousseau's notion of *pitie* in *The Second Discourse*, trans. Roger and Judith Masters (New York: St. Martin's Press, 1964), p. 102; and Aristotle's conception of "noble pleasure" derived from moral choice and in the service of justice: "There is a difference between pleasures that come from noble sources and pleasures that come from bad sources, and the pleasure of a just man cannot be felt by someone who is not just" (*Nicomachean Ethics*, book 1, 1099a, p. 20, book 10, 1174a, p. 278). Also, cf. Aristotle's *Politics*, book 3, ch. 9, p. 121 ("it is our love of others that causes us to prefer life in society").

[6]Jefferson to John Adams, February 25, 1823, *A-JL*, 2:589.

[7]Jefferson to Peter Carr, August 10, 1787, *WTJ*, 6:262.

losophers, with ethical systems premised on man's selfish desires, should subordinate their theories to the realities of man's social nature derived from the moral sense.[8]

Jefferson became especially critical of the archetypical liberal philosopher Thomas Hobbes. He considered Hobbes's conception of man a "humiliation to human nature" with its claim "that the sense of justice and injustice is not derived from our natural organization" but solely from an artificial construct designed to serve purely selfish desires through a state of entirely instrumental dimensions.[9] Jefferson's criticism of Destutt de Tracy rested on the French political economist's adherence to liberal psychology and ethics: "He adopts the principle of Hobbes, that justice is founded in contract solely. I believe, on the contrary, that it is an instinct, and innate, that the moral sense is as much a part of our natural constitution as that of feeling, seeing or hearing; as a wise Creator must have seen to be necessary in an animal destined to live in society."[10] In place of Hobbes's naturally solitary man and purely contractual justice, Jefferson offered this syllogism: "Man was created for social intercourse; but social intercourse cannot be maintained without a sense of justice; then man must have been created with a sense of justice."[11] Of course, liberalism can conceive of "civil intercourse," consisting of independent individuals persuing their own self-interest and secured by conventional (social contract) "justice"; but Jefferson, with Aristotle and Lord Kames, considered "social intercourse" as presuming an inherent social nature, providing a corollary innate sense of justice, and regarded mere conventional legal

---

[8]Thomas Jefferson, "Opinion on French Treaties," *WTJ* (Ford ed.), 6:225.

[9]Jefferson to Francis W. Gilmer, June 7, 1816, *WTJ* (mem. ed.), 15:24.

[10]Jefferson to John Adams, October 14, 1816, *A-JL,* 2:492. Joyce Appleby correctly shows Jefferson's affinity for much of Tracy's philosophy, especially his economics and criticism of Montesquieu's claim that republican governments are limited to small nations, in "What Is Still American in the Political Philosophy of Thomas Jefferson," *William and Mary Quarterly* 39 (April 1982): 287–309. This letter suggests, however, that Jefferson parted company with Tracy in the latter's adherence to liberal psychology. For Jefferson's views on Montesquieu that confirm his agreement with Tracy's critique, see his *Commonplace Book,* pp. 32–34, 267.

[11]Jefferson to Francis W. Gilmer, June 7, 1816, *WTJ* 15:25.

regulations protecting individual rights to be neither truly social nor entirely natural.

The existence of this innate capacity for justice was not invalidated, for Jefferson, by its apparent absence in some individuals: "The want or imperfection of the moral sense in some men, like the want or imperfection of the senses of sight and hearing in others, is no proof that it is a general characteristic of the species."[12] Indeed, Jefferson took man's social nature so for granted that he was more inclined to accuse God of some mistake rather than to admit its absence: "The Creator would have been a bungling artist, had he intended man for a social animal, without planting in him social dispositions."[13]

The moral conduct appropriate to this divinely ordained social nature did not, for Jefferson, consist in a primary concern with individual interests or with the building of a moral philosophy on the basis of human selfishness and greed. Rather, this innate moral quality dictated a concern for the good of others, and the whole community: "the essence of virtue is in doing good to others."[14] Of the liberal ethics of self-interested calculation, Jefferson wrote:

> I consider our relations with others as constituting the boundaries of morality. With ourselves we stand on the ground of identity, not of relation, which last, requiring two subjects, excludes self-love confined to a single one. To ourselves, in strict language, we can owe no duties, obligation requiring also two parties. Self-love, therefore, is no part of morality. Indeed, it is exactly its counterpart. It is the sole antagonist of virtue, leading us constantly by our propensities to self-gratification in violation of our moral duties to others.[15]

---

[12]Jefferson to Thomas Law, June 13, 1814, *The Complete Jefferson,* ed. Saul K. Padover (New York: Tudor, 1943), p. 1033; thus Jefferson took Aristotle's position of not defining individuals on the basis of their apparent incompleteness, but rather on the basis of their essential *telos* or complete development as human beings.

[13]Ibid. Cf. Bolingbroke's remarks in Kramnick, *Bolingbroke and His Circle,* pp. 86–89.

[14]Jefferson to John Adams, October 14, 1816, *A-JL,* 2:492.

[15]Jefferson to Thomas Law, June 13, 1814, *CJ,* pp. 1032–33. Cf. Aristotle, "this kind of just is complete virtue of excellence. . . . It is complete virtue and

Jefferson believed that this innate moral sense made just actions pleasurable,[16] but he acknowledged that this ethical sense, with its "noble pleasure," was distributed unevenly among individuals, as were the other senses.[17] As such, Jefferson found the presence of man's innate moral quality "the brightest gem with which the human character is studded, and the want of it more degrading than the most hideous of bodily deformities."[18] But where a deficiency in the moral sense was present, Jefferson had confidence in man's capacity for development through moral education.[19] Like the sense of sight and hearing, which could be refined and sharpened with training, this ethical capacity was also susceptible to instruction and cultivation. Furthermore, along with those other faculties, this moral sense could be strengthened through exercise, and refined through habitual practice.[20] Hence, Jefferson encouraged Peter Carr to "lose no occasion of exercising your dispositions to be grateful, to be generous, to be charitable, to be humane, to be true, firm, orderly,

---

excellence in the fullest sense, because it is the practice of complete virtue. It is complete because he who possesses it can make use of his virtue not only by himself, but also in his relations with his fellow men" (*Nicomachean Ethics,* book 5, 1129b–30a, p. 114).

[16]Ibid., *CJ,* p. 1033; to John Adams, October 14, 1816, *A-JL* 2:492; to Peter Carr, August 10, 1787, *WTJ,* 6:262.

[17]Ibid. *WTJ,* p. 257. This variability in capacity or development of this innate moral sense did not diminish its universality for Jefferson: In spite of other prejudices, he did not deny the moral sense to either Negroes or Indians (see *Notes on the State of Virginia,* in *CJ,* p. 664) declaring only that it seemed absent in Napoleon (to John Adams, February 25, 1823, *A-JL,* 2:589). Cf. Aristotle, references to the variable capacity for goodness (*Nicomachean Ethics,* book 2, 116, p. 34, 1109a, p. 50, book 8, 1156a–57a, pp. 218–20).

One of the best expressions of the pleasure of the moral sense sympathies is in Jefferson's famous "Head and Heart" dialogue in a letter to Maris Cosway, October 12, 1786, *The Papers of Thomas Jefferson,* 20 vols., ed. Julian Boyd (Princeton, N.J.: Princeton University Press, 1950), 10:449.

[18]Jefferson to Thomas Law, June 13, 1814, *CJ,* p. 1034.

[19]Ibid., p. 1033.

[20]Jefferson to Peter Carr, August 10, 1787, *WTJ,* 6:257. Cf. Aristotle, "virtues . . . we acquire first having put them into action. . . . we learn by doing. . . . we become just by the practice of just actions" (*Nicomachean Ethics,* book 2, 1103a–1103b, pp. 33–34). See also Boorstin, *The Lost World of Thomas Jefferson* (New York: Henry Holt, 1948), p. 146.

couragcous, ctc. Consider every act of this kind as an exercise which will strengthen your moral faculties and increase your worth."[21]

Thus for Jefferson, the moral sense which provided the basis for human society also required society for its education and development. Ethical conduct was neither simply an innate, individual matter, nor purely the responsibility of society; rather, it was both—man is born with an inherent moral capacity and political society is necessary to cultivate and perfect that potential.[22]

Jefferson placed the duty of educating individuals' moral capacities on philosophers, the clergy, and legislators.[23] And as he considered it the business of legislators to educate citizens' ethical sensibilities, politics for Jefferson could not be limited to purely liberal strictures of protecting private rights and individual interests. Rather, the moral sense, which included knowledge and choice of the good, sympathy for others' sufferings, and concern for the well-being of society generally, constituted a public sense of virtue, requiring both education and practice in political life. For Jefferson, the political structure which provided both education and practice in public life, thereby cultivating man's moral sense, was the participatory democracy of ward government.[24]

POLITICAL SOCIETY

Thomas Jefferson's political philosophy is most classically republican in his conception of political society. His emphasis on

---

[21] Ibid., *WTJ,* 6:258.

[22] Cf. Aristotle, *Nicomachean Ethics,* book 2, 1103, p. 33.

[23] Jefferson to Thomas Law, June 13, 1814, *CJ,* p. 1034.

[24] Cf. Aristotle's views on the relation between political participation and the development of individual virtue: "Lawgivers make the citizens good by inculcating [good] habits in them. . . . the main concern of politics is to engender a certain character in the citizens and to make them good and disposed to perform noble actions" (*Nicomachean Ethics,* book 2, 1103b, p. 34, book 1, 1099b, p. 23); also "a citizen is in general one who has a share both in ruling and in being ruled. . . . in the best constitution it means one who is able and who chooses to rule and be ruled with a view to a life that is in accordance with goodness" (*Politics,* book 3, ch. 13, pp. 131–32).

political participation, an economically independent and educated citizenry, a natural aristocracy of wisdom and virtue, and
the corruption of this classical republic and its balanced constitution by a centralized commercial regime, all reveal his affinity
for ideas found in Aristotle, Cicero, Montesquieu, and Harrington.[25] The center of Jefferson's classical republican theory is
his conception of ward democracy, with its educational, political,
and economic components, and its theory of leadership and
representation that leads into Jefferson's idea of federalism.[26] The
essential nature of ward government to Jefferson's vision of the
good political society was expressed in a letter of 1816: "As Cato,

---

[25] J. G. A. Pocock, "Cambridge Paradigms and Scotch Philosophers," in *Wealth
and Virtue,* eds. Istuan Hont and Michael Ignatieff (Cambridge: Cambridge
University Press, 1983), p. 236; Pocock, *Virtue, Commerce and History* (Cambridge: Cambridge University Press, 1985), pp. 41–44; Pocock, *The Machiavellian Moment* (Princeton, N.J.: Princeton University Press, 1980), p. 393;
Pocock, "Machiavelli, Harrington, and English Political Ideologies in the Eighteenth Century," *William and Mary Quarterly* 22 (October 1965): 553–65;
Gordon Wood, *The Creation of the American Republic* (Chapel Hill: University
of North Carolina Press, 1969), pp. 53–58; Lance Banning, *The Jefferson Persuasion* (Ithaca, N.Y.: Cornell University Press, 1978), pp. 29–46.

The absence of Machiavelli from this list of classical republican thinkers in-
fluencing Jefferson's political philosophy confirms the misgiving I have over his
inclusion in the paradigm, as expressed below (see Appendix). Jefferson adheres
to the traditional conception of Machiavelli as the theorist of intrigue, ruth-
lessness, and power politics, as revealed in his characterization of "the mean,
wicked and cowardly cunning of the cabinets of the age of Machiavelli" (to
William Duane, April, 1813, *WTJ,* 6:109).

[26] Jefferson's conception of small ward republics seems to be influenced by his
understanding of the Greek polis, the English hundreds, New England townships, and Indian tribes (see Matthews, *The Radical Politics of Thomas Jefferson,*
p. 83, which concurs with my placing ward democracy at the center of Jefferson's
political philosophy). Previous examinations of Jefferson's concept of ward democracy have tended to describe only one or two of these aspects, never por-
traying the comprehensive whole. For example, Adrienne Koch's *The Philosophy
of Thomas Jefferson* (Chicago: Quadrangle, 1964), ch. 18, and Hannah Arendt's
On Revolution (pp. 252–57) emphasize the political dimension at the expense
of the educational and economic; while Dumas Malone's *Jefferson and His Time:
Jefferson the Virginian,* vol. 1 (Boston: Little, Brown, 1948), ch. 20, discusses
the educational component without reference to its political and economic implications. No one has adequately linked Jefferson's theory of local ward democracy with his conception of American federalism.

then, concluded every speech with the words '*Cartago delenda est.*,' so do I every opinion, with the injunction, 'divide the counties into wards.' "[27]

(*Education*)

Into the eighteenth-century Virginian society which restricted education largely to the private tutors of wealthy children, Jefferson's original motive for establishing ward districts was to provide mass education at public expense. His "Bill for the More General Diffusion of Knowledge" (1779) proposed dividing each county into wards or "hundreds" of sufficient size and population (five to six square miles and one hundred citizens) to support an elementary school. At this level, the essentials of reading, writing, and arithmetic, along with history (ancient and modern) were to be taught to all children, at the public expense, for three years.[28]

The next level of public education would reside in county grammar schools, where Latin, Greek, English, geography, and the higher mathematics would be taught. Each year, "impartial examinations" would be administered to those children completing their elementary course to determine which, among the "best and most promising genius and disposition" (but too poor to afford it) would proceed to these classical grammar schools at public tuition. Then, out of each county grammar school class, the single best student would be selected annually to continue his education for four years longer, at public expense. From among the graduates of this elite group, the best 50 percent would continue to be supported by the public while attending the university, where "all the useful sciences" (from physics to philosophy, ethics and economics) would be taught them for three years.[29]

---

[27]Jefferson to Joseph Cabell, February 2, 1816, *WTJ*, 14:423. Also, to Major John Cartwright, June 5, 1824, *WTJ*, 16:46.

[28]In *CJ*, pp. 1049, 1065; see also Jefferson, *Notes on the State of Virginia*, pp. 667–68; and Matthews, *The Radical Politics of Thomas Jefferson*, pp. 82, 88.

[29]*CJ*, pp. 1052–54, 667, 1065. Cf. Plato's rigorous and impartial educational

The final purpose of this elaborate educational system was to collectively cultivate the individual's innate capacities, and to thereby promote a more just and harmonious society. "The general objects of this law," Jefferson said, "are to provide an education adapted to the years, to the capacity, and to the condition of everyone and directed to their freedom and happiness" by developing the "worth and genius" in the people regardless of "wealth, birth or other accidental condition."[30] It was essential for the system to be publicly financed in order to cultivate "those talents which nature has sown as liberally among the poor as the rich, but which perish without use, if not sought for and cultivated."[31] As such, in this system, Jefferson believed "the principal foundations of future order will be laid."[32] Therefore, the universal public education of that "future order" was not conceived by Jefferson to merely provide equality of private op-

---

process in *The Republic,* book 3, 413d–414a, book 4, 429a, book 6, 487a. For more on Jefferson's proposed educational system, see letter to Peter Carr, September 7, 1814, *CJ,* p. 1065; to John Adams, Oct. 28, 1813, *A-JL,* 2:389; and to Governor John Tyler, *WTJ,* 12:393.

This applied only to white males. Jefferson gave little attention to public education for blacks and women (Boorstin, *The Lost World of Thomas Jefferson,* p. 224), both being essentially disenfranchised. For white women, Jefferson recommended training in "dancing, drawing and music," as these would enhance their gracefulness and contribute to their domestic charms (see letter to N. Burwell, 1818, *WTJ,* 7:101).

[30] Jefferson, *Notes on the State of Virginia,* p. 667.

[31] Thomas Jefferson, Bill for the More General Diffusion of Knowledge, *CJ,* p. 1048. Thus, Jefferson's belief in the equal distribution of virtue and talents among all classes of children did not imply the absolute equality of those qualities of every child; and here Jefferson resembles Plato more than scholars have cared to admit. Jefferson may not have spoken of intrinsic differences in individual capacities (or of the possibility of gifted parents producing undistinguished offspring and vice-versa) in Plato's terms ("The Myth of the Metals") but he did divide society, for educational purposes, into classes of "laboring and learned," which were both presumably natural and discerned and developed through a discriminating educational system; see Jefferson to Peter Carr, September 7, 1814, *CJ;* and Plato's *Republic,* book 3, 415a–d.

[32] Jefferson, *Notes on the State of Virginia, CJ,* p. 667. This does not mean that such a virtue, served by public education, was incompatible, for Jefferson, with economic advancement (see Joyce Appleby, *Capitalism and a New Social Order* [New York: New York University Press, 1984], pp. 14–15).

portunity (as it has come to be perceived), but was designed to serve the public good. Hence, Jefferson's conception of the public good is not reducible to the sum of private goods.

He noted in his *Commonplace Book* on Montesquieu's *Spirit of the Laws*: "He considers political virtue . . . as the energetic principle of a democratic republic . . . and shews that every government should provide that its energetic principle should be the object of the education of its youth."[33] In Jefferson's view, the educational system grounded in ward districts contributed to the public good by (1) educating the populace sufficiently to participate directly in local community affairs and to intelligently select political leaders and representatives; and (2) by providing advanced learning to those capable of receiving it, i.e., those possessed of "virtue and wisdom," and who therefore are well suited to being chosen as political leaders and representatives. Thus public education of the whole people was to secure the public happiness of all classes of society.[34]

---

[33] Jefferson, *Commonplace Book,* p. 259. The relevant passages from Montesquieu, *Spirit of the Laws,* trans. Thomas Nugent (New York: Hafner Press, 1975), 1:33–34, follow:

> It is in a republican government that the whole power of education is required. The fear of despotic governments naturally arises of itself amidst threats and punishments; the honor of monarchies is favored by the passions, and favors them in its turn; but virtue is a self-renunciation, which is ever arduous and painful.
>
> This virtue may be defined as the love of the laws and of our country. As such love requires a constant preference of public to private interest, it is the source of all private virtues; for they are nothing more than this very preference itself.
>
> This love is peculiar to democracies. In these alone the government is intrusted to private citizens. Now, a government is like everything else: to preserve it we must love it.

See also David W. Carrithers, "Montesquieu, Jefferson and the Fundamentals of Eighteenth-Century Republican Theory," *The French-American Review* 4 (Fall 1982).

[34] Cf. Plato's particularized education serving the universal good: "in founding the city we are not looking to the exceptional happiness of any one group among us, but, as far as possible, that of the city as a whole" (*The Republic,* book 4, 420b). I am not suggesting that Jefferson got this idea from what he called "the whimsies, puerilities, and unintelligible jargon" of Plato's *Republic* (letter to John

For Jefferson, an "ignorant democracy" was a contradiction in terms ("If a nation expects to be ignorant and free, in a state of civilization, it expects what never was and what never will be")[35]; but a populace educated in ward schools might intelligently participate in its own self-governance: "Every government degenerates when trusted to the rulers. . . . The people themselves therefore are its only safe depositories. And to render even them safe, their minds must be improved."[36]

Concurrent with the ward schools' elevation of the masses to a level commensurate with democratic participation, the advanced levels of Jefferson's system provided students of "wisdom and virtue" with successively more rigorous standards of scholarship in order to produce a pool of superior minds and dispositions from which the people could select able governors and representatives of a just and happy state.[37] Jefferson clearly explained this intended political effect of his educational structure in the preamble of his "Bill for the More General Diffusion of Knowledge":

> Whereas it is generally true that people will be happiest whose laws are best, and are best administered, and that laws will be wisely formed, and honestly administered, in proportion as those who form and administer them are wise and honest; whence it becomes expedient for promoting the public happiness that those persons, whom nature hath endowed with genius and virtue, should be rendered by liberal education worthy to receive and able to guard the sacred deposit of the rights and liberties of their fellow citizens,

---

Adams, 1814, *WTJ*, 6:354), only that there appear to be some similarities in their conceptions of education.

[35] Jefferson letter to Charles Yancey, *WTJ*, 6:517.

[36] Jefferson, *Notes on the State of Virginia*, p. 668; see also Jefferson, Bill for the More General Diffusion of Knowledge, p. 1048; and Jefferson's letter to Monsieur A. Coray in which he encourages French leaders to elevate the masses by "improving their minds and qualifying them for self-government" (October 31, 1823, *WTJ*, 15: 481).

[37] Jefferson's emphasis on a public dimension of happiness in what follows reveals his classical republican bent, as opposed to the purely private, individualistic "happiness" of liberalism, and gives clues to his substitution of "happiness" for "property" in the Declaration of Independence. Wood, *The Creation of the American Republic*, pp. 72–75, discusses the place of education in republican ideology.

and that they should be called to that charge without regard to wealth, birth, or other accidental condition or circumstance; but the indigence of the greater number disabling them from so educating, at their own expense, those of their children whom nature hath fitly formed and disposed to become useful instruments for the public; it is better that such should be sought for and educated at the common expense of all, than that the happiness of all should be confined to the weak or wicked.[38]

Jefferson's appreciation of public education properly serving the good of society rather than personal ambition was extended to his conception of teachers. The grammar school teachers were to be selected, in Jefferson's view, not merely on the basis of their scholarly abilities, but also for their "fidelity to the Commonwealth" and its republican principles.[39] With similar regard for the political side of the teacher's role, Jefferson recommended to the trustees of a Tennessee college the "esteem, respect and gratitude due to those who devote their time and efforts to rendering the youths of every successive age fit governors for the next."[40] And of George Wythe's tenure as Professor of Law at William and Mary College, Jefferson wrote: "Wythe's school is numerous. They hold weekly courts. . . . The professors join in it, and the young men dispute with elegance, method and learning. This single school, by throwing from time to time new hands well-informed into the Legislative, will be of infinite value."[41]

Thus, with its concern for qualifying the populace for self-government, cultivating leaders of wisdom and virtue, and seeing teachers as contributing to these political ends, Jefferson regarded

---

[38]Cf. James Harrington's educational system (*Oceana,* ed. S. B. Liljegren [Westport, Conn.: Hyperion Press, 1979], p. 168): "And the formation of a Citizen in the Womb of the Common-wealth is his Education. That which is proposed for the erecting and endowing of Schools throughout the Tribes capable of all the Children of the same, and able to give unto the Poor the Education of theirs *Gratis,* is only matter of direction in the case of very great Charity, as easing the needy of they Charge of their Children from the ninth to the Fifteenth year of their Age."

[39]Jefferson, Bill for the More General Diffusion of Knowledge, p. 1052.

[40]Jefferson to Hugh L. White et al., May 6, 1810, *WTJ,* 12:388.

[41]Jefferson to James Madison, 1780, *WTJ* (Ford ed.), 2:322.

his education system as genuinely "public." He considered this system, along with the direct democracy of the ward districts, as constituting the "two great measures . . . without which no republic can maintain itself."[42] For Jefferson believed that the division of counties into wards for educational purposes would soon also serve political purposes, providing the geographical boundaries for small, local, participatory democracies: "My partiality for that division is not founded in views of education solely, but infinitely more as the means of a better administration of our government, and the eternal preservation of its republican principles."[43]

Politics

Jefferson's ward districts bore a striking resemblance to the ideal Greek polis, which also strove to realize man's social nature through direct citizen participation in local community life.[44] As such, classical republics were necessarily limited in size and population, so Jefferson adapted them to the large American continent through an original theory of representative democracy which grew out of, rather than competed with, ward divisions.[45]

---

[42]Jefferson to Gov. John Tyler, May 26, 1810, *WTJ* (mem. ed.), 12:393; see also Jefferson to Joseph C. Cabell, Jan. 31, 1814, *WTJ*, 14:84 ("There are two objects, indeed, which I shall claim a right to further as long as I breath, the public education, and the substitution of counties into wards. I consider the continuance of republican government as absolutely hanging on these two hooks").

[43]Jefferson to Gov. Wilson C. Nicholes, April 2, 1816, *WTJ*, 14:454; and as Jefferson wrote to Joseph C. Cabell of the wards (February 2, 1816, p. 423): "Begin them only for a single purpose; they will soon show for what others they are the best instruments."

[44]Jefferson's "mixed" response to Montesquieu's theories revolve around his attempt to adapt classical small republics to a large country, which the French philosopher insisted could not be done (see Jefferson, *Commonplace Book,* pp. 32–33, 267). When Jefferson served in France, he also found that parties favorable to monarchy cited Montesquieu, which further cooled Jefferson's attitude (see Appleby, "What Is Still American"). That which Jefferson retained of Montesquieu was his most classical republican qualities: emphasis on civic virtue, public participation, small republics, public education, and an economic dimension to democracy.

[45]Cf. Aristotle, *Politics,* book 1, ch. 6, 9, pp. 114, 121; that Jefferson was

Having declared the wards to be "small republics," created out of the smallest existing jurisdictions, the counties, Jefferson provided a precise definition of his notion of these political entities: "Were I to assign to this term a precise and definite idea, I would say, purely and simply, it means a government by its citizens in mass, acting directly and personally, according to rules established by the majority; and that every other government is more or less republican in proportion as it has in its composition more or less of this ingredient of the direct action of the citizens."[46]

Among those things which Jefferson considered immediately relevant to ward residents in addition to the elementary schools, and well within their competence, were "care of their poor, their roads, police, elections, the nomination of jurors, administration of justice in small cases, elementary exercises of militia and all those concerns which, being under their eye, they would better manage than the larger republics of the county or state."[47]

---

familiar with Aristotle's *Politics* is evidenced by the presence of the book on his bedside table late in his life (see Merrill D. Peterson, *Thomas Jefferson and the New Nation* [New York: Oxford University Press, 1970], p. 1008).

[46] Jefferson to John Taylor, May 28, 1816, *WTJ*, 15:19; to Samuel Kercheval, July 12, 1816, p. 33 ("let it be agreed that a government is republican in proportion as every member composing it has his equal voice in the direction of its concerns"). Cf. Montesquieu, "The people, in whom the supreme power resides, ought to have the management of everything within their reach; that which exceeds their abilities must be conducted by their ministers" (*Spirit of the Laws*, 1:9).

Such participatory democracy, with its capacity for creative action and adaptation to change, provides, in my view, for the "perpetual revolution" which Richard Matthews argues is central to Jefferson's political thought (*The Radical Politics of Thomas Jefferson*). Additionally, the famous "earth belongs to the living" letter to James Madison (September 6, 1789), on which Matthews bases much of his argument, refers literally to the earth as landed property, which Jefferson sought to distribute to all citizens as a requisite to classical republican citizenship.

[47] Jefferson to John Adams, October 28, 1813, *A-JL*, 2:390; also to Samuel Kercheval, July 12, 1816, *WTJ*, 15:37. Jefferson's vision of "social welfare," largely detailed in his *Notes on the State of Virginia*, differs substantially from both contemporary (late twentieth century) national welfare programs and the local private charities which existed throughout America prior to the New Deal. And, while not as technologically sophisticated as the former, they seem rather closer in humanitarianism to the latter, while still being publicly supported. For

Such minor republics, which Jefferson saw as akin to New England townships, were for him "the wisest invention ever devised by the wit of man for the perfect exercise of self-government, and for its preservation,"[48] because "by making every citizen an acting member of the government, and in the offices nearest and most interesting to him, will attach him by his strongest feelings to the independence of his country, and its republican Constitution."[49] And while he saw direct participation in local political life drawing out citizens' affections for their community and its public virtue, Jefferson also regarded the wards' small size as contributing to public deliberation and the development of citizens' minds, as evidenced by his repeated plea: "reduce your legislature to a convenient number for full but orderly discussion."[50]

In addition to cultivating the citizens' hearts and minds, classical participatory democracy would also prevent the degeneration of the state into a tyranny; for Jefferson warned: "If [the people] become inattentive to the public affairs, you and I, Con-

---

example, care of the poor, aged, and sick was to be publicly subsidized (through ward revenues) but privately administered, always attempting to supplement the family and friendship relations that already existed. The sick who had no family or friends with whom to stay were to be placed in the home of a "good farmer," whose family environment Jefferson considered more conducive to healing than an impersonal hospital: "Nature and kind nursing save a much greater proportion in our plain way, at a smaller expense, and with less abuse" (in *CJ*, p. 658).

[48] Jefferson to Samuel Kercheval, July 12, 1816, *WTJ*, 15:38.

[49] Ibid., p. 37. Cf. this to Aristotle's definition of citizenship: "there are different kinds of citizens, but . . . a citizen in the fullest sense is one who has a share in the privileges of rule" (*Politics,* book 3, ch. 5, p. 112).

[50] Jefferson to Samuel Kercheval, July 12, 1816, *WTJ*, 15:36. This also reflects Jefferson's mature appreciation of classical political theory, as does his comment to Monsieur Coray that "Greece was the first of civilized nations which presented examples of what man should be" (see entire letter). Other evidence for Jefferson's attitudes toward modern conflictual and ancient consensual politics appears in his *Autobiography,* where he contrasts the American Congress's "very contentious . . . morbid rage of debate" with the young French aristocrats in Paris during the late 1780s, whose "coolness and candor of argument . . . logical reasoning and chaste eloquence, disfigured by no gaudy tinsel of rhetoric or declamation, and truly worthy of being placed in parallel with the finest dialogues of antiquity, as handed to us by Xenophon, Plato, and Cicero" (pp. 70, 114).

gress and Assemblies, Judges and Governors, shall all become wolves."[51] In other words, for Jefferson, democratically educated citizens are the best insurance against government violations of individual natural rights: "when there shall not be a man in the State who will not be a member of some one of its councils great or small, he will let the heart be torn out of his body sooner than his power be wrested from him by a Caesar or a Bonaparte."[52]

Still, in spite of Jefferson's devotion to small, classical republics, he was not blind to their geographical limitations. "Such a government," he wrote, "is evidently restrained to very narrow limits of space and population."[53] In a country the size of the United States, therefore, Jefferson conceived of a kind of representative democracy as a natural extension of ward republican government. "This I should consider as the nearest approach to a pure republic, which is practicable on a large scale of country or population."[54] But unlike the immediate structure of ward republics, which might benefit from notions borrowed from Ancient Greece, this

---

[51] Jefferson to Col. Edward Carrington, January 16, 1787, *WTJ*, 5:58. Boorstin, for whom Jefferson's political philosophy provides no positive form of community or moral dimension, but only natural rights protection from state power, emphasizes what he calls this "prophylatic" purpose of democracy (*The Lost World of Thomas Jefferson*, pp. 190–95).

[52] Jefferson to Joseph C. Cabell, Feb. 2, 1816, *WTJ*, 14:422. The same argument for the strength of republican government occurs in Jefferson's "First Inaugural Address": "It is the only one where every man, at the call of the laws, would fly to the standard of the law, and would meet invasion of the public order as his own personal concern" (in *CJ*, p. 385).

[53] Jefferson to John Taylor, May 28, 1816, *WTJ*, 15:19. Cf. Aristotle's observation in *Politics*, book 7, ch. 5, p. 266; and Montesquieu's *Spirit of the Laws*, 1:120:

It is natural for a republic to have only a small territory; otherwise it cannot long subsist. In an extensive republic there are men of large fortunes, and consequently of less moderation.

In an extensive republic the public good is sacrificed to a thousand private views; it is subordinate to exceptions, and depends on accidents. In a small one, the interest of the public is more obvious, better understood, and more within the reach of every citizen; abuses have less extent, and, of course, are less protected.

[54] Jefferson to John Taylor, ibid.

representative adaptation of local participatory democracy to a large nation required entirely original ideas: "The full experiment of a government democratical, but representative, was and is still reserved for us. . . . this . . . has rendered useless almost everything written before on the structure of government; and in a great measure, relieves our regret, if the political writings of Aristotle, or of any other ancient, have been lost, or are unfaithfully rendered or explained to us."[55]

Jefferson provided an entirely new political theory; but his original theory, designed for the unique conditions of America, still drew heavily from the past. He constructed this larger, representative republic out of the smaller, participatory republics, insisting that "these little republics would be the main strength of the great one."[56] The means of connecting the local ward republics with the increasingly centralized republics will be discussed at length below, but its general principle is that the elementary republics of the wards, the county and state republics, and the republic of the Union, would form a system of fundamental checks and balances for the government,[57] founded on every citizen personally taking part in the administration of the public affairs.[58]

This Jeffersonian standard of American federalism provided the basis for his critique of what became the existing structure of American constitutional government. What remains for him of republicanism after the Federalists' manipulation of Constitution and Court "is not the fruit of our Constitution, but has prevailed in spite of it."[59]

Thus, Jefferson consistently regarded the classical ward republics as "the key-stone of the arch of our government."[60] His

---

[55] Jefferson to Isaac Tiffany, August 26, 1816, ibid., p. 66; though even here, evidence exists showing that Jefferson's idea of the states' "compact" into a federated Union may have been an attempt at replicating the "confederation" of Greek city-states, of which Athens was a part (see his notes on Stanyan's *Grecian History* (1739) in *Commonplace Book,* entries 717, 729.

[56] Jefferson to Gov. John Tyler, May 26, 1810, *WTJ,* 12:394.

[57] Jefferson to Joseph C. Cabell, February 2, 1816, *WTJ,* 14:422.

[58] Jefferson to Samuel Kercheval, July 12, 1816, *WTJ,* 15:35.

[59] Ibid.

[60] Jefferson to John Adams, Oct. 28, 1813, *A-JL,* 2:390.

concept of small participatory democracies constituted his mature political theory, and his conception of human nature as naturally social and requiring the exercise of one's moral and political faculties for individual development and for the public good generally, contrasted with his earlier, revolutionary theory premised in Lockean liberalism. And yet, just as his revolutionary appeal to Lockean categories defended autonomous, republican legislatures, Jefferson's later appeal to classical republican politics, he believed, would enhance the preservation of fundamental rights and liberties. From his mature perspective, Jefferson did not emphasize the individual's freedom from social ties, but rather, insisted that the absence of an active public realm cultivating man's social and moral capacities would not lead to freedom and happiness but to "sinning and suffering." Apart from a meaningful public life, Jefferson believed, individuals would be reduced to miserable "automatons" devoid of true, intelligent choice.[61] This left Jefferson, just two years before his death at age 83, still working for an amendment to Virginia's Constitution dividing the counties into ward republics.[62]

Economics

A lively controversy has existed over the place of economics in Jefferson's political philosophy and whether he fits within or outside the classical republican paradigm.[63] My view is that Jefferson's emphasis upon economic independence as requisite to a democratic citizenry and criticism of economic manipulation (public credit, stockjobbing, financial imperialism) place him

---

[61] Jefferson to Samuel Kercheval, July 12, 1816, *WTJ*, 15:40. For a contemporary discussion of such "sinning and suffering," see Benjamin R. Barber, *Strong Democracy: Participatory Politics for a New Age* (Berkeley: University of California Press, 1984). Barber also argues that direct democracy may better protect individual rights than a purely Lockean, limited representative state.

[62] By the time of his retirement, Jefferson was not optimistic over the likelihood of reforming the American federal structure, believing that the "golden moment is past for reforming these heresies" of the republican creed (to John Taylor, May 28, 1816, *WTJ*, 15:22).

[63] Joyce Appleby, *Capitalism and a New Social Order*; Appleby "What Is Still American"; Pocock, *The Machiavellian Moment*.

within the classical republican paradigm, but his affinity for certain kinds of economic development and free market commerce belie any "nostalgic" country ideology. Basically, we find that where Jefferson saw economics contributing to independent citizens and an independent nation, he approved of them; and where he saw economic policies detracting from an independent, educated, and politically active citizenry and self-sufficient republic, he opposed them. Hence, Joyce Appleby's claim that Jefferson was not against economic development, may not be inconsistent with his classical republican politics.

Jefferson considered the economic reforms which he proposed in Virginia shortly after returning from Philadelphia as integral to his conception of ward democracy. These economic policies supported Jefferson's educational and political structures by providing the material self-sufficiency and independence for the community of citizens to develop their social faculties and participate in self-government. Jefferson's Virginia reforms were to accomplish this by (1) eliminating the oligarchy of concentrated wealth along with its exclusive hold on political activity; and (2) elevating the mass of citizens to economic independence, making them capable and interested in public participation.[64]

Jefferson hoped to pull down the oligarchy of concentrated wealth by abolishing the laws of primogeniture and entail. Both primogeniture (which preserved large estates by restricting inheritance to the eldest son) and entail (which prohibited the division and sale of estates) dated from a time when a threatened feudal nobility sought to protect itself from the rising moneyed classes. Jefferson, like those new classes that strove to break up the old aristocracy with either armed forces or market forces, hoped to dissolve the Virginia oligarchy's preeminent control over the land and its corresponding monopoly over public affairs.[65] But unlike those other critics of the landed nobility who

---

[64] Cf. Aristotle on the relation between politics and economics: "Now property is part of a household and the acquisition of property part of the economics of a household; for neither life itself nor the good life [i.e., politics] is possible without a certain minimum standard of wealth" (*Politics,* book 1, ch. 4, p. 3).

[65] See Jefferson to John Adams, Oct. 28, 1813, *A-JL,* 2:389, 391; Jefferson, The Bill to Abolish Entails (1776), in *CJ,* p. 88; and Jefferson, *Autobiography,* pp. 50–57.

wished simply to eliminate the oligarchy's predominant position by transferring its power and wealth to themselves, Jefferson proposed redistributing that landed property and influence among the population generally, providing the people with an economic independence commensurate with respectable participation in the life of the republic.

In his "Proposed Constitution for Virginia" (1776), Jefferson included a provision for establishing relative economic equality: "Every person of full age neither owning nor having owned [50] acres of land, shall be entitled to an appropriation of [50] acres or so much as shall make up what he owns or has owned [50] acres in full and absolute dominion."[66] So, after Harrington, Jefferson believed that because political power followed property ownership, a virtuous republic must have an economically independent citizenry and general equality of condition in moderate wealth.[67] Hence, in his *Commonplace Book,* Jefferson noted Montesquieu's dictum: "In a democracy, equality and frugality should be promoted by the laws . . . by laying burthens on the richer classes and encouraging the poorer ones."[68]

---

[66] In *CJ,* p. 109; Jefferson understood the corollary requisite of such property in the strict regulation of immigration (see *Notes on the State of Virginia,* pp. 624–26).

[67] Drew McCoy, *The Elusive Republic: The Political Economy in Jeffersonian America* (Chapel Hill: University of North Carolina Press, 1980), p. 67; Banning, *The Jeffersonian Persuasion,* p. 29.

[68] Jefferson, *Commonplace Book,* p. 259. Jefferson, like Aristotle, and unlike Plato, preferred to keep economics a private or "household" matter rather than a purely private (a la Plato's communism) matter; but, recognizing the public implications of private property, Jefferson sought to preserve a rough equality of wealth, very much like Rousseau's famous statement: "By equality, we should understand, not that the degrees of power and riches are to be absolutely identical for everybody, but that power shall never be great enough for violence; and shall always be exercised by virtue of rank and law; and that, in respect to riches, no citizen shall ever be wealthy enough to buy another, and none poor enough to be forced to sell himself . . . allow neither rich men nor beggars. These two estates, which are naturally inseparable, are equally fatal to the common good" (*The Social Contract,* trans. G. D. H. Cole [New York: Dutton, 1977], p. 204). Cf. Montesquieu (*Spirit of the Laws* 1:41–42): "The good sense and happiness of individuals depend greatly upon the mediocrity of their abilities and fortunes. Therefore, as a republic, where the laws have placed many in a middling station, is composed of wise men, it will be wisely governed; as it is composed of happy

This is why Jefferson was so shocked at the extremes of wealth and poverty in prerevolutionary France, as he detailed in a letter to James Madison (October 28, 1785) after giving money to a beggar woman:

> She burst into tears of a gratitude which I could perceive was unfeigned. . . .
>
> This little *attendrissement*, with the solitude of my walk led me into a train of reflections of that unequal division of property which occasions the numberless instances of wretchedness which I had observed in this country and is to be observed all over Europe. The property of this country is absolutely concentrated in a very few hands, having revenues of from half a million of guineas a year downwards . . .
>
> I asked myself what could be the reason that so many should be permitted to beg who are willing to work, in a country where there is a very considerable proportion of uncultivated lands? These lands are kept idle mostly for the sake of game . . .
>
> I am conscious that an equal division of property is impracticable. But the consequences of this enormous inequality producing so much misery to the bulk of mankind, legislators cannot invent too many devices for subdividing property, only taking care to let their subdivisions go hand in hand with the natural affections of the human mind . . .
>
> Another means of silently lessening the inequality of property is to exempt all from taxation below a certain point, and to tax the higher portions of property in geometrical progression as they rise. Whenever there is in any country uncultivated lands and unem-

---

men, it will be extremely happy"; and Harrington (*Oceana,* p. 17): "You have Aristotle full of it in divers places, especially where he saith that Immoderate Wealth, as where One man or the Few have greater possessions than equality or the frame of the Common-wealth will bear, is an occasion of Sedition, which ends for the greater part in Monarchy; and that for this cause the Ostracisms hath been received in divers places, as in *Argos* and *Athens.* But that it were better to prevent the growth in the beginning, then, when it hath gotten head, to seek the remedy of such an evil." See also Aristotle (*Politics,* book 9, ch. 11, pp. 171–72): "cities have every chance of being well-governed in which the middle class is large, stronger if possible than the other two together, or at any rate stronger than one of them. For the addition of its weight to either side will turn the balance and prevent the extravagances of the opposition. For this reason it is a happy state of affairs when those who take part in the life of the state have a moderate but adequate amount of property."

ployed poor, it is clear that the laws of property have been so far extended as to violate natural right. The earth is given as a common stock for man to labour and live on. If, for the encouragement of industry we allow it to be appropriated, we must take care that other employment be furnished to those excluded from the appropriation. If we do not the fundamental right to labour the earth returns to the unemployed. It is too soon yet in our country to say that every man who cannot find employment but who can find uncultivated land, shall be at liberty to cultivate it, paying a moderate rent. But it is not too soon to provide by every possible means that as few as possible shall be without a little portion of land. The small landholders are the most precious part of a state.[69]

Jefferson's view that farmers are "the most precious part of a state" is well known, but its relation to his political theories is less well developed. It is the landowner's economic independence that produces his public virtue and qualifies him for political participation.

Those who labour in the earth are the chosen people of God, if ever he had a chosen people, whose breasts he has made his peculiar deposit for substantial and genuine virtue. It is the focus in which he keeps alive that sacred fire, which otherwise might escape from the face of the earth. Corruption of morals in the mass of cultivators is a phenomenon of which no age nor nation has furnished an example. It is the mark set on those, who not looking up to heaven, to their own soil and industry, as does the husbandman, for their subsistence, depend for it on the casualties and caprice of customers. Dependence begets subservience and venality, suffocates the germ of virtue, and prepares fit tools for the designs of ambition.[70]

---

[69] A similar letter to Madison in 1787, when Jefferson was again writing from France, develops his famous "earth belongs to the living" theme again urging the redistribution of landed property every generation through legal means (see Matthews, *The Radical Politics of Thomas Jefferson,* ch. 2).

[70] Jefferson, *Notes on the State of Virginia,* p. 678. Cf. Aristotle (*Politics,* book 6, ch. 4, p. 240): "An agricultural population makes the best demos; so that it is in fact possible to make a democracy anywhere where the population subsists in agriculture or stock-raising and pastures"; and Harrington (*Oceana,* p. 169): "Agriculture is the Bread of the Nation, we are hung upon it by the teeth; it is a mighty Nursery of Strength, the best Army, and the most assured Knapsack; it is managed with the least turbulent or ambitious, and most innocent hands of all other Arts. Wherefore I am of Aristotle's opinion, That a Common-wealth of Husband-men (and such is ours) must be the best of all others."

Jefferson even encouraged Virginia farmers to plant wheat instead of tobacco because it was easier to grow and would allow greater leisure for public participation and virtue.[71]

His hatred for the "mobs of the cities" was not due to a purely anti-urban bias (he loved Paris), but rather that the "ignorance, poverty and vice" of city dwellers disqualified them for wise, independent, and virtuous political participation.[72] Power in the hands of European city mobs, Jefferson wrote to Adams, "would be instantly perverted to the demolition and destruction of everything public and private."[73] When later in his life Jefferson modified his agrarian ideal to accommodate domestic cities and manufacturers, it was again to secure economic independence — this time for the nation:

> We must now place the manufacturer by the side of the agriculturist.
> . . . Shall we make our own comforts, or go without them, at the will of a foreign nation? He, therefore, who is against domestic manufacture must be for reducing us either to dependence on that foreign nation or to be clothed in skins, and to live, like wild beasts, in dens. . . . I am not one of these; experience has taught me that manufacturers are now as necessary to our independence as to our comfort."[74]

Jefferson's mature appreciation of "a due balance between agriculture, manufactures and commerce,"[75] producing national independence, now required a citizen with economic independence either in land ownership or a "satisfactory situation," to maintain a qualified democratic citizenry and a virtuous republic.

---

[71]T. H. Breen, "The Culture of Agriculture: The Symbolic World of the Tidewater Planter, 1760–1790," in *Saints and Revolutionaries*, eds. David Hall, John Murrin, and Thad Tate (New York: Norton, 1984), pp. 183–84.

[72]Jefferson to John Adams, Oct. 28, 1813, *A-JL*, 2:391. Cf. Aristotle (*Politics*, book 6, ch. 4, pp. 242–43): "Their lives are inferior, and the work they do has not the quality of goodness; they are mere labourers, hirelings, the most ordinary specimens of humanity."

[73]Jefferson, ibid. Elsewhere Jefferson contrasted "the rabble" of France with the "steady and rational" citizens of America, again attributing this difference, in part, to their respective economic circumstances (see *The Anas*, in *CJ*, p. 1213).

[74]Jefferson to Benjamin Austin, January, 1816, *WTJ*, 6:521.

[75]Jefferson to Thomas Leiper, 1809, *WTJ*, 5:417.

As he wrote to John Adams in 1813: "Everyone, by his property, or by his satisfactory situation, is interested in the support of law and order. And such men may safely and advantageously reserve to themselves a wholesome control over their public affairs."[76]

Jefferson's criticism of Hamilton and the Federalists' policies, as we shall see, centered around their corruption of this classical republican balance, by concentrating political power in the central government (as opposed to the states and localities) and concentrating economic power in the hands of a few wealthy merchants and bankers (through policies of paper money, public credit, stockjobbing, etc.). For Jefferson, as for other classical republican thinkers, there was a constant struggle between a corrupt centralized government that wished to control all wealth and power (giving it out as patronage to control the masses) and a strong, independent, democratic citizenry capable of ruling itself with wisdom, virtue, and self-respect. His economically independent, publicly educated, and politically experienced citizens would be capable of self-governance and strong enough to resist the manipulations and encroachments of a Federalist administration. But to complete this virtuous republic in the large American continent, Jefferson had to devise a system for leadership, representation, and federalism compatible with ward democracy and worthy of a free people.

Leadership and Representation

Jefferson believed that the public education, political participation, and economic equality entailed in ward democracy would

---

[76]Jefferson, *A-JL* 2:391. Cf. Aristotle: "the government of a state is rule over free and equal persons" (*Politics,* book 1, ch. 6, p. 37); this would have led him to question any socialist politics which reduce all politics merely to reflections of economic activity. The ancients considered the satisfaction of material needs as freeing the individual to participate in community life for its own sake: "[Political] life is action, not production" (*Politics,* book 1, ch. 4); "a state is something more than an investment; its purpose is not merely to provide a living but to make a life that is worthwhile. Otherwise, a state might be made up of slaves or animals, and that is impossible, because slaves and animals are not free agents and do not participate in well-being" (book 3, ch. 9, p. 119).

create the conditions necessary for an intelligent electorate to select the best individuals in society to represent these small republics at the county, state, and federal levels of American government. Those individuals, suited to governing the nation beyond the area of the small ward republics, were called by Jefferson "the natural aristocracy,"[77] distinguished by their "genius and virtue" or "wisdom and goodness," as the most appropriate source of political leadership for a well-ordered and just republic:[78] "The natural aristocracy I consider as the most precious gift of nature for the instruction, the trusts, and the government of society."[79] Jefferson went so far as to say that his entire theory of ward democracy implied: "May we not even say that that form of government is the best which provides the most effectually for a pure selection of these natural aristoi in the offices of government?"[80]

This Jeffersonian conception of the best leadership residing in a natural aristocracy of wisdom and goodness flows directly from Jefferson's understanding of "nature" with respect to human nature (that man is naturally a social, ethical being) and its extension into the political realm may be best expressed in this syllogism: Man is naturally social; the social qualities are wisdom

---

[77] For the alternative standards of aristocracy (heredity and wealth) in Jefferson's time, see Kramnick, *Bolingbroke and His Circle*, pp. 82–83; and Kramnick, "Republican Revisionism Revisited," pp. 653, 660.

[78] Jefferson, A Bill for The More General Diffusion of Knowledge, p. 104; Jefferson to John Adams, October 28, 1813, *A-JL*, 2:389. See also Jefferson's reference to the "wisdom and virtue" of the national legislature in his "First Inaugural Address," p. 384. Cf. Plato, *The Republic*, book 1, pp. 350, 354c, book 4, 428a–d, 445d, book 6, 487a, book 9, 582d–83a. Jefferson may have complained of the "whimsies" of Plato's *Republic* (see letter to John Adams, *A-JL*, 2:432), but his theory of rulership by a wise and virtuous aristocracy, cultivated through a systematic and rigorous education, bears a striking resemblance to the platonic conception of just rule by the "wise and good" (i.e., philosophers) raised in a careful and discriminating educational process. Indeed, he complains less of the platonic doctrine itself than of its "unintelligible jargon" (p. 432) and of its "mysticisms incomprehensible to the human mind" (Jefferson to William Short, October 13, 1819, *WTJ*, 15:219).

[79] Jefferson to John Adams, October 28, 1813, *A-JL*, 2:388.

[80] Ibid. (Plato would have thought so; see *The Republic*, book 4, 428a–d, 445d, book 9, 528d–83a.)

and virtue; hence, the most wise and good man is the best and most natural, or the natural aristocrat. That is, by creating and preserving the just and wise society, the natural aristocrat produces the conditions which enable the citizens to best realize their true nature as social beings, justice and harmony being necessary to complete and happy social relations; and the natural aristocrat himself is the highest expression of that just order, recognized and nurtured by its educational system, and returning in rulership to reinforce the society which developed him.[81] As Jefferson said of the natural aristocracy, in a manner reminiscent of man's divinely-ordained social nature (the moral sense): "indeed it would be inconsistent in creation to have formed man for the social state, and not to have provided virtue and wisdom enough to manage the concerns of the society."[82]

Jefferson carefully distinguished between this natural aristocracy, with its positive effects on society, and the artificial or "pseudo" aristocracy, founded on wealth and birth without either virtue or talents, and its destructive effects on society:[83] "The artificial aristocracy is a mischievous ingredient in government and provision should be made to prevent its ascendency."[84]

---

[81] Cf. Plato's *Republic*, book 4, 428a, book 6, 487a.

[82] Jefferson to John Adams, October 28, 1813, *A-JL*, 2:387 (Jefferson added, quoting Theognis: "good men never harmed any city," p. 390).

[83] For John Adams, wealth and birth defined the natural aristocracy: "There are a few in whom all these advantages of birth, fortune, and fame are united. . . . the natural aristocracy . . . forms a body of men which contains the greatest collection of virtues and abilities" (John Adams, *A Defense of the Constitutions of the United States*, 1787, in Kenneth Dolbeare, *American Political Thought* [Monterey: Duxbury Press, 1981], p. 76); "Now, my Friend, who are the [aristocrats]? Philosophy may Answer 'The Wise and Good.' But the World, Mankind, have by their practice always answered, 'The rich the beautiful and well born' " (Adams to Jefferson, September 2, 1813, *A-JL*, 2:371; see also Adams to Jefferson, Nov. 15, 1813, 398).

[84] Jefferson to John Adams, Oct. 28, 1813, ibid., p. 388; see also Jefferson's remark to George Washington: "I hold it to be one of the distinguishing excellences of elective over hereditary successions, that the talents which nature has provided in sufficient proportion, should be selected by the society for the government of their affairs, rather than that this should be transmitted through the loins of knaves and fools [i.e., monarchs], passing from the debauches of

Jefferson's mature democratic theory was such a provision. Living at a historical moment halfway between feudal monarchy and capitalist democracy, Jefferson saw, with uncommon acumen, that if the aristocracy of wisdom and virtue did not govern in America, politics would necessarily be dominated by one or the other "tinsel" aristocracies: either the aristocracy of birth (feudal heredity) or the aristocracy of wealth (capitalist power), neither of which was capable of producing the just republic necessary to the fulfillment of man's social nature. Jefferson's idea of classical ward republics connected successively to more centralized republics within the federal structure through representatives drawn from the natural aristocracy of wisdom and virtue was an attempt to prevent the ascendency of either "pseudo" aristocracy.[85]

This natural aristocracy, drawn from and elected by the common people, was a "golden mean" between an oppressive hereditary aristocracy and the radically egalitarian populist democracy that rejected all aristocracy, even of virtue and merit.[86]

---

the table to those of the bed" (in *CJ*, p. 275).

John Adams was suspicious of the people's capacity to overcome its envy of superiority (even of virtue and talents) long enough to wisely choose them as leaders: "The Greeks in their Allegorical Style said that the two Ladies [Aristocracy] and [democracy], always in a quarrel, disturbed every neighborhood with their brawls" (Adams to Jefferson, July 13, 1813, *A-JL*, 2:355); and "The people have almost always expected to be served gratis and be paid for the honor of serving them; and their applauses and adorations are bestowed too often on artifices and tricks, on hypocrisy and superstition, on flattery, bribes, and largesses" (Adams, *A Defense of the Constitutions of the United States*, p. 70).

Jefferson may have been more sanguine over the citizenry's capacity to choose the natural aristocracy for leadership positions because Virginia had a tradition of popular deference to an educated, public-spirited gentry (see Joy B. and Robert R. Gilsdorf, "Elites, and Electorates: Some Plain Truths for Historians of Colonial America," in Hall, Murrin and Tate, *Saints and Revolutionaries*, p. 210).

[85] With respect to the alternative ruling aristocracies, cf. Plato, *The Republic*, book 9, 582d–83a. For a strikingly similar discussion of the true aristocracy (i.e., the rule of the best, or most possessed of wisdom, virtue and talents), see Aristotle's *Politics*, book 3, chs. 13, 15, 17; of its "pseudo" imitators in wealth and birth, book 3, ch. 12; and of their inappropriate claims to virtue, *Nicomachean Ethics*, book 4, 1124a–b.

[86] Montesquieu described this radically egalitarian tendency in a democracy

The Tory reactionaries wanted no aristocracy but that of heredity and family; the rich Federalists wanted no aristocracy but that of wealth; and the radical democrats wanted no aristocracy at all. Jefferson's natural aristocracy of wisdom and virtue, serving the good of the whole society, drawn from and elected by an economically independent, educated, and politically experienced citizenry, provided a balanced, moderate conception of democratic leadership and representation.

Jefferson went to his grave confident that with the people properly prepared and qualified—educationally, economically, and politically—this country would not have to suffer under the unjust rule of the false aristocracies of birth or wealth, as the citizens would have among them men of wisdom and goodness, and would themselves be wise enough to recognize them. The ward republics "would have raised the mass of the people to the high ground of moral respectability necessary to their own safety, and to orderly government; and would have completed the great object of qualifying them to select the veritable aristoi, for the trusts of government, to the exclusion of the Pseudalists."[87]

(*The Spirit of the Laws*, 1:111–12): "As distant as heaven is from earth, so is the true spirit of equality from that of extreme equality. The former does not imply that everybody should command, or that no one should be commanded, but that we obey or command our equals. It endeavors not to shake off the authority of a master, but that its masters should be none but its equals."

[87]Jefferson to John Adams, October 28, 1813, *A-JL*, 2:390.

CHAPTER 5

JEFFERSONIAN FEDERALISM:
THEORY AND PRACTICE

THE CLASSICAL republican paradigm seems most persuasive in its description of Jefferson's conception of federalism. Here it illuminates the Jeffersonian "Country" agrarian virtue attacking the Hamiltonian Federalist "Court" corruption based in financial manipulation through the National Bank, stockjobbing, public credit, and centralized administration.[1] Yet, we find that even in this classic Court-Country battle, Jefferson invokes Lockean language reminiscent of his earlier revolutionary writings, now in defense of the sovereign autonomy of state and local republics against the encroachment of a distant centralized and corrupt regime. While in the 1770s, that distant, oppressive regime was in London, usurping the legitimate rule of the colonial legislatures, in the 1790s and 1820s, it was in Washington, where under the control of the "Federalists," it was usurping the legitimate rule of the state and local republics. So, even where

---

[1] J. G. A. Pocock, "Machiavelli, Harrington, and English Political Ideologies in the Eighteenth Century," *William and Mary Quarterly* 22 (October 1965): 549–83, see esp. 565–70; Pocock, ed., *Three British Revolutions, 1641, 1688, 1776* (Princeton, N.J.: Princeton University Press, 1980), pp. 5–14; Lance Banning, *The Jeffersonian Persuasion* (Ithaca, N.Y.: Cornell University Press, 1978), pp. 128–74; John Murrin, "The Great Inversion, Or Court versus Country," in *Three British Revolutions*, pp. 385–427.

Jefferson's classical republicanism is most obvious—in his conception of the autonomy of classical participatory republics governed by an economically independent, educated, and politically active citizenry, promoting public virtue within a balanced, mixed constitution—we find it complemented by a modified Lockean liberalism declaring the rights of equal and independent legislatures.

WARD DEMOCRACY
AND THE CONSTITUTION

An interesting pattern emerges in the texts of Jefferson's major letters concerning ward democracy.[2] In these letters, a common sequence of ideas may be discerned which connect Jefferson's mature political theory with his conception of the Constitution and American federalism: (1) a general description of ward democracy and its manifold benefits; (2) a delineation of the proper relationship between the small ward republics and the increasingly centralized republics on the county, state, and national levels of government; (3) a sudden shift to a seemingly abstract discussion of the necessity, in all societies, to periodically alter the Constitution (Jefferson recommends changing them every generation, insisting that "laws and institutions must go hand in hand with the progress of the human mind");[3] (4) an enumeration of specific suggestions for reforming the existing American Constitution, in order to maintain its correct federal structure and republican principles (indicating an erosion of Jefferson's confidence in the constitutional provisions he originally believed would guarantee state and local sovereignty—the Bill of Rights, especially the Tenth Amendment, and Article IV, Section 4).[4]

---

[2] See Jefferson to Monsieur Coray, Oct. 31, 1823, *The Writings of Thomas Jefferson,* 20 vols., ed. Albert Ellery Bergh (Washington, D.C.: Thomas Jefferson Memorial Assoc., 1904–05), 15:488; to Major John Cartwright, June 5, 1824, *WTJ,* 16:42–52; and to Samuel Kercheval, July 12, 1816, *WTJ,* 15:32–44.

[3] Jefferson to Samuel Kercheval, ibid.

[4] Jefferson's initial acceptance of the U.S. Constitution was premised on the legitimate expectation that Article IV, Section 4 ("The United States shall guar-

JEFFERSON'S FEDERAL REPUBLIC

Jefferson's standard for American federalism was a functional standard: each tier of government was to perform those functions that it did best. And in Jefferson's eighteenth-century view, this standard distributed domestic concerns to the state and local governments, restricting the national government primarily to matters of foreign relations.[5]

[T]he way to have good and safe government, is not to trust it all to one, but to divide it among the many, distributing to every one exactly the functions he is competent to. Let the national government be entrusted with the defense of the nation, and its foreign and federal relations; the State governments with the civil rights, laws, police, and administration of what concerns the State generally; the counties with the local concerns of the counties; and each ward direct the interests within itself. It is by dividing and subdividing these republics from the great national one down through all its subordinations, until it ends in the administration of every man's farm by himself; by placing under everyone what his own eye may superintend, that all will be done for the best.[6]

---

antee to every State in this Union a Republican Form of Government") and the Tenth Amendment ("the powers not delegated to the United States by the Constitution, nor prohibited by it to the States, are reserved to the State respectively, or to the people") would ensure the existence of state and local sovereignty apart from the national government, and that those decentralized authorities would be participatory ("republican") democracies of the kind he saw in southern wards and New England townships.

[5]Jefferson to Joseph C. Cabell, February 2, 1816, *WTJ*, 14:421. Jefferson's criticism of Aristotle and Montesquieu was not over their conceptions of man's social nature or the need for political participation by a virtuous citizenry, but rather their contention that such a classical republic could only exist in a small nation, while Jefferson believed that it could exist in a large nation if connected in this way to successively more centralized republics. Of Aristotle and the Greeks, Jefferson wrote, "They know no medium between a democracy (the only pure republic, but impractical beyond the limits of a town) and an abandonment of themselves to an aristocracy, or a tyranny independent of the people. It seems not to have occurred to them that where the citizens can not meet to transact their business in person, they alone have the right to choose the agents who shall transact it; and that in this way a republican, or popular government, of the second grade of purity, may be exercised over any extent of country" (to Isaac Tiffany, 1816, *WTJ*, 7:32).

[6]Jefferson, *The Commonplace Book of Thomas Jefferson: A Repertory of His Ideas*

This distribution of the government into the national (one) the states (few), and the localities (many) formed Jefferson's conception of a balanced, mixed Constitution.

Thus, Jefferson's federal republic was a pyramid founded upon the local ward republics, topped by county and state republics, and crowned by the national republic, which formed a graduation of authorities constituting a system of checks and balances for the government.[7] Hence, Jefferson's famous inaugural phrase, "We are all republicans—we are federalists,"[8] becomes something more than a conciliatory remark; it constitutes a concise description of his conception of American federalism, elaborated in a political diary of the period: "I fondly hope, 'we may now truly say, we are all republicans, all federalists,' and that the motto of the standard to which our country will forever rally, will be, 'federal union, and republican government.' "[9] The extent to which Jefferson subordinated the "federal" to the "republic" is illustrated by his insistence that this pyramid of republics be "cemented" by direct participation of every citizen in the political life of the country.[10]

Because this classical democracy in the ward republics constituted the foundation of the Federated Union, and because the local and state republics were charged with most domestic political concerns, the national government, properly relegated to international affairs, was approached by Jefferson with Lockean language reminiscent of his revolutionary writings, protecting those elemental republics from inordinate encroachment by the centralized government. That is, while the direct control of internal politics (cultivation and exercise of man's moral sense, effective ordering of education, economics, and leadership, etc.)

---

on Government, ed. Gilbert Chinard (Baltimore: Johns Hopkins Press, 1926), pp. 32–34, 37, 267.

[7] Jefferson to Joseph C. Cabell, Feb. 2, 1816, *WTJ,* 14:422. See C. B. Macpherson, *The Life and Times of Liberal Democracy* (New York: Oxford University Press, 1977), pp. 108–109.

[8] Jefferson, "First Inaugural Address," *The Complete Jefferson,* ed. Saul K. Padover (New York: Tudor, 1943), p. 385.

[9] See Jefferson, *The Anas, CJ,* pp. 1212–13.

[10] Jefferson to Samuel Kercheval, July 12, 1816, *WTJ,* 15:38.

made classical participatory politics appropriate to state and local regimes, the distant and removed quality of the national government made liberal political principles (limited government, delegated authority) appropriate to the federal government. This explains why Jefferson, after developing an extensive and even somewhat intrusive role for the local ward democracies (strictly regulating education, politics, economics, and leadership) nevertheless characterized good federal government as very limited, as evidenced in his often misinterpreted remark in the first inaugural address: "a wise and frugal government, which shall restrain men from injuring one another, which shall leave them otherwise free to regulate their own pursuits of industry and improvement."[11] Jefferson was content to limit the national government in this liberal fashion because he was confident that Americans' political life was best conducted in the local and state republics. As he insisted in his first message to Congress, "the states themselves have principal care of our persons, our property, and our reputation, constituting the great field of human concerns."[12]

Not the least of these human concerns for Jefferson was the cultivation of the individual's moral sense, that highest faculty of man, which required the intimacy of local education and political participation for its development and exercise. Therefore, when Jefferson perceived the federal government encroaching upon the local ward and state republics through increasing involvement in domestic concerns, his assaults on that national authority came in the language of Locke, and called for a restrained, limited government in a manner strongly reminiscent of his revolutionary writings directed against the British Parliament's similar encroachment on the local colonial legislatures. In both instances, the freedom defended with Lockean rhetoric

---

[11] In Jefferson, *CJ*, p. 386.

[12] Ibid., p. 390. See also The Kentucky Resolutions (1798), in which Jefferson makes the distinction between the national and the state governments in these terms: "a general government for special purposes—delegated to that government certain definite powers, reserving, each state to itself the residuary mass of right to their own self-government" (*CJ*, p. 129).

was the freedom of small communities to exercise self-govern-ment, and of individuals to realize their social nature through participation in and control over their collective lives. Since, as we have seen, Jefferson regarded an economically independent citizenry as requisite to a virtuous republic that was not only a defense of political balance, but also a defense of evenly distrib-uted property against Hamilton's financial schemes that would concentrate wealth in the hands of a few.

JEFFERSON'S SECOND
DECLARATION OF INDEPENDENCE

A few months before his death, in December of 1825, Jefferson wrote "The Solemn Declaration and Protest of the Common-wealth of Virginia, On the Principles of the Constitution of the United States of America, And On The Violations of Them."[13] Its liberal phraseology echoes Jefferson's first Declaration of In-dependence: He again refers to "free and independent" states, to the "usurpation" of their sovereign authority by a centralized power, and he again appeals to his "federal brethren" to discon-tinue these encroachments while noting the threat to "life, liberty and property" implied in their invasion of state and local de-mocracy.[14]

The kinship of this second declaration with its revolutionary predecessor is apparent even in its preamble: "The States in North America which confederated to establish their independence of the government of Great Britain, of which Virginia was one, became, on acquisition, free and independent States, and as such authorized to constitute governments, each for itself, in such form as it thought best."[15] After recounting the historical origins

---

[13] Ibid., pp. 134–36.

[14] Ibid. Cf. Jefferson's language in the original Declaration of Independence: "free and independent" states; "usurpation"; "British brethren"; "life, liberty."

[15] Thomas Jefferson, The Solemn Declaration And Protest Of The Common-wealth Of Virginia, On The Principles Of The Constitution Of The United States Of America, And On The Violations Of Them (December 1825), *CJ*, p. 134.

of the states' independence from Great Britain, Jefferson provided his explanation of the creation of a new central authority in America, through the compact made by those independent states: "They entered into a compact (which is called the Constitution Of the United States of America), by which they agreed to unite in a single government as to their relations with each other, and with foreign nations. . . . They retained at the same time, each to itself, the other rights of independent government, comprehending their domestic interests."[16] But, as the British Parliament before it, this newly-created federal government gradually extended its authority into the economic, social, and political prerogatives of the smaller republics: "[t]he federal branch has assumed in some cases, and claimed in others, a right of enlarging its own powers . . . which this assembly [of Virginia] does declare to be usurpations of the power retained to the independent [State] branches."[17]

As with the British Parliament, it was not merely the expansion of the federal government which threatened local democracy, it was the corruption of politics itself, following from the commercial venality to which distant regimes were particularly susceptible and which threatened to poison public virtue by removing the government from direct citizen accountability and delivering it to self-seeking speculators and merchants. Political corruption originally attributed to the "greed and avarice" of English merchants,[18] Jefferson now saw emanating from "the wealthy aristocrats, the [American] merchants connected closely with England [and] the newly created paper fortunes."[19] Hence, Jefferson could write of the rule of the High Federalists, and especially their leader Alexander Hamilton, "all the administrative

---

[16] Ibid.

[17] Ibid., p. 135. Jefferson saw this usurpation by the federal government generally, but especially by the executive and judicial branches (see Murrin, "The Great Inversion" pp. 405–406, 427; Robert E. Shalhope, "Thomas Jefferson's Republicanism and Antebellum Southern Thought," *Journal of Southern History* 42 (November 1976): 529–55, at 545.

[18] See Thomas Jefferson, *A Summary View of the Rights of British America, The Papers of Thomas Jefferson,* 60 vols., ed. Julian Boyd (Princeton, N.J.: Princeton University Press, 1950), 1:124, 127.

[19] Jefferson, *The Anas,* p. 1258.

laws were shaped on the model of England . . . and [were] to be warped, in practice, into all the principles and pollutions of their favorite English model. . . . [For] Hamilton was not only a monarchist, but for a monarchy bottomed in corruption."[20]

Jefferson's own definition of "corruption" as "a legislature legislating for its own interests, in opposition to those of the people" followed Aristotle's definition of a corrupt regime ruling for its private good rather than for the public good.[21] Such corruption, for the Greeks as for Jefferson, flourished in a distant regime, where leaders were less directly accountable to the people. There a government might be captured by commercial interests, who because of their necessity to constantly be occupied with private gain, were not well suited to protecting the good of the whole society, the public virtue. Jefferson's system of participatory republics, producing both an educated electorate and a natural aristocracy capable of perceiving the good of the whole society, was designed to diminish the possibility of rule by the "pseudo-aristocracy" of wealth which brought such corruption to the public realm. As Lance Banning has pointed out, the real threat of this political and financial corruption to the public virtue was the concentration of wealth and political power which would effectively destroy the economically independent and politically active citizenry whose function was necessary to a classical republic.[22]

---

[20] Ibid., pp. 1210–11, 1226 (Jefferson concluded that "Hamilton was, indeed, a singular character").

[21] Aristotle, *The Politics,* book 3, chs. 6, 7.

[22] Banning, *The Jeffersonian Persuasion,* p. 150. As Jefferson wrote of the Federalists: They wish "to lessen the dependence of the Executive and of one branch of the Legislature on the people, some by making them hold for life, some hereditary, and some even giving the Executive an influence by patronage or corruption over the remaining popular branch, so as to reduce the elective franchise to its minimum" (to J. F. Mercer, 1804, *WTJ,* 4:563). Cf. Harrington (*Oceana,* ed. S. B. Liljegen [Westport, Conn.: Hyperion Press, 1979], p. 37):

> such (except it be in a city that has little or no land, and whose revenue is in trade) as in the population or balance of dominion or property in land, such is the nature of the empire.
> If one man be sole landlord of a territory, or overbalance the people, for

But American federalism developed in a rather different way from Jefferson's ideal vision, breeding an isolated and venal federal legislature which Jefferson identified largely with Hamilton's fiscal system and the corruption it symbolized. The Secretary of Treasury's plans for reimbursing holders of government bonds, for assuming the state's debts, and for establishing a National Bank all revealed this commercial corruption; Jefferson regarded the lot as a "base scramble" for public funds and misappropriated political power, a "detestable game" of "greedy creditors and speculators" whose manipulations of the public trust allowed "immense sums to be filched from the poor and ignorant."[23]

---

example three parts in four . . . his empire is absolute monarchy.

If the few or a nobility, or a nobility with the clergy be landlords, or overbalance the people to the like proportion, it makes the *Gothic* balance . . . and the empire is mix'd monarchy . . .

And if the whole people be landlords, or hold the lands so divided among them, that no one man, or number of men, within the compass of the *few* or *aristocracy*, overbalance them, the empire (without the interposition of force) is a commonwealth.

[23]Jefferson, *The Anas,* pp. 1208, 1246. Cf. Bolingbroke's characterization of Walpole's government dominated by "the usurer and the stockjobbers . . . those leeches who fill themselves continually with the blood of the nation" (in Isaac Kramnick, *Bolingbroke and His Circle* [Cambridge, Mass.: Harvard University Press, 1968], p. 37). Jefferson went so far as to advocate secession by the southern states rather than be dominated by the financial policies of the Northeast:

Every society has a right to fix the fundamental principles of its association, and to say to all individuals, that, if they contemplate pursuits beyond the limits of these principles, and involving dangers which the society chooses to avoid, they must go somewhere else for their exercise; that we want no citizens, and still less ephemeral and pseudo-citizens, on such terms. We may exclude them from our territory, as we do persons infected with disease. Such is the situation of our country. We have the most abundant resources of happiness without ourselves, which we may enjoy in peace and safety, without permitting a few citizens, infected with the mania of rambling and gambling, to bring danger on the great mass engaged in innocent and safe pursuits at home. In your letter to Fisk, you have fairly stated the alternatives between which we are to choose: 1, licentious commerce and gambling speculations for a few, with eternal war for the many; or, 2, restricted commerce, peace, and steady occupations for all. If any State in the Union will declare that it prefers separation with the first alternative, to a contin-

And, worse, Hamilton's corrupting fiscal policy derived from a corrupt political theory, which strove to govern men by appealing solely to their private interests, and expected to somehow create a just and orderly society out of the aggregate of those interests, rather than acknowledging and cultivating the highest faculty in man: his social, ethical nature. For Jefferson, Hamilton's policies came directly from this base, Hobbesian view of human nature. Hamilton's fiscal system "had two objects; 1st, as a puzzle, to exclude popular understanding and inquiry; 2d, as a machine for the corruption of the legislature; for he avowed the opinion, that man could be governed by one of two motives only, force or interest; force he observed, in this country was out of the question, and the interests, therefore, of the members [of Congress] must be laid hold of, to keep the legislative unison with the executive."[24] Thus, Hamilton's politics were not "evil" as such; they were merely the logical extension of a psychology which had dominated modernity since Hobbes, that conceives of man as only a material individual, seeking nothing but self-preservation; but once one constructs a polity on the basis of such a limited view of human nature, it becomes a kind of self-fulfilling prophesy, as men are forced to confirm to it out of self-defense. This, Jefferson pointed out, is precisely what happened: "And with grief and shame it must be acknowledged that [Hamilton's] machine was not without effect; that even in this, the birth of our government, some members were found sordid enough to bend their duty to their interests, and to look after personal rather than public good."[25]

---

uance in union without it, I have no hesitation in saying, "let us separate." I would rather the States would withdraw, which are for unlimited commerce and war, and confederate with those alone which are for peace and agriculture. (to William Crawford, June 20, 1816, *WTJ*, 11:538)

This alienation from northern commercial corruption extended to southerners being educated in New England, which was one of the reasons Jefferson wanted to establish the University of Virginia, providing southern gentlemen with an alternative to Princeton or Harvard (see Shalhope, "Thomas Jefferson's Republicanism," p. 552).

[24] Jefferson, *The Anas*, p. 1208.

[25] Ibid. Jefferson elsewhere described Mr. Hamilton as "a man whose history, from the moment history can stoop to notice him, is a tissue of machinations

The ultimate effect of this corrupt system, premised in a corrupt political theory founded on a corrupt psychology, was to debase political leaders and followers alike. Instead of the rule of the natural aristocracy of wisdom and virtue, emanating from participatory ward republics, Hamilton's system, and the perversions it symbolized, issued forth the rule of "the stock-jobbing herd,"[26] reducing public good to the sum of private goods. This, in turn, replaced the active, intelligent citizenry of Jefferson's vision, with an alienated, passive and dangerously ignorant populace obsessed with private ambition. Jefferson blamed this dismemberment of the body politic on policies committed to withdrawing the people from honest business pursuits and encouraging them to "occupy themselves and their capitals in a species of gambling, destructive of morality, and which has introduced its poison into the government itself."[27]

Rather than the virtue and wisdom created by the democracy of the ward republics flowing up to the higher regions of American federalism, Jefferson sadly observed the corruption and venality of Hamilton's federal government filtering down to pollute the state and local regimes. Jefferson's attacks on the federal structure and the Constitution grew out of that witness.

By the end of his life, Jefferson's political theory had come full circle. The Lockean liberalism of his early, revolutionary writings, superseded by the classicism of his mature political thought, appeared again in his final writings concerning American federalism. And yet, while a Lockean or classical perspective may seem to have dominated during these particular periods, the other worldview was always, at least partially, present in the background, providing the closest example of a real synthesis of liberalism and republicanism yet found. When invoking Lockean language of freedom, equality, and independence with respect

---

against the liberty of the country which has not only received and given him bread but heaped honors on his head" (quoted in Merrill D. Peterson, *Thomas Jefferson and the New Nation* [New York: Oxford University Press, 1970], p. 474). The evidence for Hamilton's uncommonly close ties with English mercantilist fortunes and their Parliament was pervasive for Jefferson (see *The Anas*, pp. 1272, 1274, 1276, 1279).

[26] Ibid., *The Anas*, p. 1210.

[27] Ibid., p. 1216.

to the British Empire or the federal government, it was on behalf of autonomous, decentralized republics; and when presenting a strong case for self-sufficient, virtuous, participatory classical republican citizens, it was with the belief that they provided the best protection against violations of individual rights and liberties.[28]

FEDERALISM IN REALITY: JEFFERSON AS PRESIDENT

Perhaps the real measure of Jefferson's conception of federalism was his conduct as president. How did he view national power and executive prerogative when he was in a position to benefit from them? Alexander Hamilton had always claimed that Jefferson would not be averse to a strong presidency, once he was in control of that office, and John Quincy Adams insisted that Jefferson's conduct of the presidency proved that his ideal republic of small decentralized democracies was something of a pose.[29]

Generally, Jefferson's policies during his two terms as president remained true to his republican ideals of protecting an independent democratic citizenry and encouraging political participation in decentralized government. His reduction of internal debt and taxes reduced economic burdens on the virtuous yeoman class; his scaling back on the army and navy, along with emphasizing the value of the militia, reinforced states' control over the military; and his reduction of federal executive patronage positions and their attendant "corruption" restored authority to the legislative branch of national government. Jefferson's principal biographer, Dumas Malone, characterized his presidency

---

[28] John Taylor of Caroline County, Virginia, a close political ally of Jefferson's, expresses a similar synthesis of liberalism and republicanism. See Garrett Ward Sheldon, *The Political Thought of John Taylor* (Lawrence: University Press of Kansas, forthcoming 1992), ch. 2.

[29] Peterson, *Thomas Jefferson and the New Nation,* pp. 691, 782; Dumas Malone, *Jefferson and His Time: Jefferson the President, First Term,* vol. 4 (Boston: Little, Brown, 1970), p. 353.

as "designed to minimize government while democratizing it, and to lighten the burdens and enlarge the freedom of the citizenry."[30] Certainly these policies were consistent with Jefferson's liberal republican ideals.

However, in two policy areas, those surrounding the Louisiana Purchase and the Embargo, Jefferson has been accused of violating his own political principles by assuming powers for the executive and the national government beyond their legitimate constitutional purview. These violations he justified alternately on the basis of expediency and the broader national interest, but his loose "construction" of the Constitution to accomplish these noble ends justified means contrary to his constitutional interpretation of strictly delegated powers to the president and the federal government, and thereby may have compromised his entire political theory. They certainly made it easier for subsequent presidents, who had fewer classical republican scruples, to expand the powers of the federal executive while citing the example of the great democrat Jefferson.

The Louisiana Purchase

Jefferson had long hoped for the establishment of an "empire of liberty" throughout the North American and South American continents, protecting his ideal liberal republicanism from the decadence, corruption, and oppression of Europe.[31] His first opportunity to realize this dream came during his first term as president when, through a series of exceedingly complex negotiations with Spain, France, and Britain, the United States acquired the "immense uncharted country" between the Mississippi and the Rocky Mountains.[32] This land acquisition virtually doubled the size of the country at a cost of $15,000,000 or about 13.5 cents an acre. The brilliance of this accomplishment, which for Jefferson removed the "greatest danger to our peace," was

---

[30]Malone, ibid., p. 239.
[31]Peterson, *Thomas Jefferson and the New Nation,* p. 745.
[32]Ibid., p. 760.

dimmed by his knowledge that it exceeded the limits of the Constitution and the executive power.[33]

Jefferson was well aware that the U.S. Constitution contained no specific authority for the federal government to acquire territory and his "strict constructionism" and sensitivity to presidential usurpation of power placed him in an awkward position vis-à-vis the Louisiana Purchase. To complicate matters further, President Jefferson received conflicting advice from his cabinet members. The attorney general claimed that only the Union of 1787 was sanctioned in the Constitution and that an amendment was required to allow acquisition of new territory and incorporation of new states.[34] Secretary of Treasury Gallatin, however, argued that as a sovereign nation, the United States could acquire territory by treaty and govern it directly or, with congressional action, incorporate it into the Union.[35] Jefferson accepted Gallatin's view on the grounds of expediency, but wished a constitutional amendment to confirm his strong federal executive action. "You are right," he wrote Gallatin, "there is no constitutional difficulty as to the acquisition of territory, and whether, when acquired, it may be taken into the Union by the Constitution . . . will become a question of expediency." Still, Jefferson added the caveat: "I think it will be safer not to permit the enlargement of the Union but by amendment of the Constitution."[36] He immediately drafted such an amendment, claiming that "the executive in seizing the fugitive occurrence which so much advances the good of this country have done an act beyond the Constitution."[37] But, when Spain and France threatened to renege on the deal and a debate over the constitutionality of the Purchase would have given them a pretext for pulling out, Jefferson again argued for expediency, urging speedy congressional action confirming the Louisiana "treaty."[38] As he wrote

---

[33] Malone, *Jefferson the President, First Term,* p. 311.
[34] Peterson, *Thomas Jefferson and the New Nation,* p. 770.
[35] Malone, *Jefferson the President, First Term,* pp. 311–12.
[36] In Peterson, *Thomas Jefferson and the New Nation,* p. 770.
[37] Ibid.
[38] Malone, *Jefferson the President, First Term,* pp. 315–17.

to James Madison, "I infer that the less we say about constitutional difficulties respecting Louisiana the better, and that what is necessary for surmounting them must be done sub silentio."[39]

As Merrill Peterson has noted, the Federalist advocates of "implied" constitutional powers would "weep at their timidity" compared to this Jeffersonian coup.[40] Years later, John Quincy Adams described the purchase of Louisiana as "an assumption of implied power greater in itself and more comprehensive in its consequences than all the assumptions of implied powers in the years of the Washington and Adams Administrations put together."[41] But Jefferson justified his actions around the Louisiana Purchase as necessary for protecting the nation from belligerent European neighbors and was willing to subordinate the letter of the law to the spirit and welfare of the republic:

> A strict observance of the written law is doubless *one* of the high duties of a good citizen, but it is not *the highest*. The laws of necessity, of self-preservation, of saving our country when in danger are of higher obligation. To lose our country by a scrupulous adherence to written law, would be to lose the law itself, with life, liberty, property and all those who are enjoying them with us; thus absurdly sacrificing the end to the means.[42]

Still, he did not abandon, in his crucial circumstances, his principles of strict adherence to delegated constitutional powers and republican procedure: "When an instrument admits two constructions, the one safe, the other dangerous, the one precise, the other indefinite, I prefer that which is safe and precise. I had rather ask an enlargement of power from the nation where it is found necessary, than to assume it by a construction which would make our powers boundless."[43]

Once the tortuous Louisiana Purchase was accomplished, the manner in which the large territory was to be governed by the

---

[39] Ibid., p. 316.
[40] Peterson, *Thomas Jefferson and the New Nation*, p. 771.
[41] Malone, *Jefferson the President, First Term*, p. 331.
[42] Jefferson to John B. Colvin, in Malone, *Jefferson the President, First Term*, p. 320.
[43] Jefferson to W. C. Nicolas, ibid., p. 318.

Jefferson Administration raised further questions about his republican ideals in practice. A Jeffersonian Congress passed the Enabling Act, which empowered the president to take possession of the Louisiana territory and vested him with full authority over all civil and military matters. This made the old Federalist attempts at a "monarchical" executive pale to insignificance and caused them to dub Jefferson the "Grand Turk."[44] But Jefferson's initial plan for governance in Louisiana, which relied on a presidentially appointed governor, secretary, and judges, grew from his belief that (as in ward republics) citizens had to be qualified for democratic self-government. Louisiana culture and politics were completely undemocratic—imbued with Spanish feudalism, Roman Catholicism, and an absence of public education.[45] Jefferson's view was that people under such conditions were as unprepared for self-governance "as children" and this was confirmed by Louisiana Governor Claiborne's observation that democratic principles were "utterly beyond their comprehension."[46] The appropriate policy in such a situation was to gradually introduce democratic practices as the people became capable of receiving them, beginning with basic civil rights: "the habeas corpus, the freedom of press, freedom of religion, etc. . . . [and then] draw their laws and organization to the mould of ours by degrees as they find practicable. . . . In proportion as we find the people there riper for receiving these first principles of freedom, Congress may from session to session confirm their enjoyment of them."[47]

John Quincy Adams argued that this treatment of Louisiana residents violated basic principles of the "consent of the governed" and the "no taxation without representation" ideals on which the American Revolution was fought.[48] He denounced

---

[44] Peterson, *Thomas Jefferson and the New Nation*, p. 777.

[45] Ibid., pp. 780, 778–79.

[46] Malone, *Jefferson the President, First Term*, pp. 349, 354. These views obviously paralleled Jefferson's attitudes toward freed blacks and the liberated French, who similarly "are not yet ripe for receiving the blessings to which they are entitled" (p. 349).

[47] Jefferson memorandum, ibid., p. 350.

[48] Ibid., p. 353.

Jefferson's hypocrisy in condemning Federalist violations of republican principles while denying them in the acquisition and governance of Louisiana:

> It gives despotic power over territories purchased. It naturalizes foreign territories in a mass. It makes French and Spanish laws a large part of the laws of the Union. It introduced whole systems of legislation abhorrent to the spirit and character of our institutions, and all this done by an administration which came in blowing a trumpet against implied powers. After this, to nibble at a bank, a road, a canal . . . was but glorious inconsistency.[49]

This inconsistency was felt by the residents of Louisiana, particularly those "middle-class" elements that felt qualified to rule themselves. Edward Livingston wrote a memorial to Congress enumerating grievances in a style reminiscent of colonial protests aimed at George III a generation earlier. Much to Jefferson's embarrassment, he now found himself in the place of the "tyrant," by violating those "fundamental, indefensible, self-evident and eternal" rights and facing the difficult question: "Do political axioms on the Atlantic become problems when transferred to the shores of the Mississippi?"[50]

The local resistance to Jefferson's plan for gradual democratization of Louisiana eventually led him, and Congress, to accept more immediate measures for representative government in the territory, along the lines of the Northwest Ordinance. In the end, this confirmed his view that "no constitution was ever before so well calculated as ours for extensive empire and self government."[51]

The Embargo

In his second term as president, Jefferson's devotion to his republican ideals of decentralized authority were called into question again, through his formulation and implementation of the embargo.

---

[49] In Peterson, *Thomas Jefferson and the New Nation*, p. 782.
[50] Ibid., p. 784.
[51] Malone, *Jefferson the President, First Term*, pp. 362–63.

Jefferson encouraged Congress to pass the Embargo
which provided a self-blockade of the United States' internal commerce, prohibiting American shipping to foreign
and foreign shipping into American ports. This freeze on
all international trade was in response to British and French
maritime wars, which subjected American ships and seamen to
confiscation and impressment. The Embargo affected about
1,500 American ships, 20,000 seamen, and $60,000,000 worth
of cargo.[52]

Originally, Jefferson saw the embargo as a policy of limited
duration necessitated by America's military weakness in defending its worldwide shipping. Later, however, Jefferson began to
see the embargo as a grand experiment, an alternative to war
that might continue indefinitely. Given the tremendous sacrifices
it placed on the American people, especially in the South, Jefferson's biographers fault him for failing to make the reasons for
such an extreme policy clear to the nation.[53] He gave no proclamation or "clarion call" to rally the people around a policy
which increasingly exercised government "control over the economic affairs of individuals that was without precedent."[54] And
as Jefferson became more enthusiastic over the benefits of the
embargo, especially the restrictions on foreign fashions and luxuries (unbecoming to "virtuous and faithful citizens") he became
increasingly fervent over the legal enforcement of the Embargo.[55]
This included constitutionally questionable search and seizure
practices toward suspected smugglers and federal dictates to
states' governors over enforcement procedures.[56] The president's
direct intervention in embargo enforcement caused Federalist
critics to call him "Thomas the First."[57] However, continued

---

[52] Peterson, *Thomas Jefferson and the New Nation,* pp. 883–84.

[53] Malone, *Jefferson and His Time: Jefferson the President, Second Term,* vol. 5 (1974), pp. 483, 487; Peterson, *Thomas Jefferson and the New Nation,* p. 884.

[54] Malone, ibid., pp. 487, 590.

[55] Peterson, *Thomas Jefferson and the New Nation,* pp. 886–87.

[56] Malone, *Jefferson the President, Second Term,* pp. 595, 603; Peterson, ibid.

[57] Malone, ibid., p. 486.

British aggression against American shipping silenced most criticism of the embargo, which even won the support of Jefferson's nemesis, John Quincy Adams, who endorsed the government's regulation of individual private property in almost Rousseauian terms: "[It is] an experiment to see how far the Government might calculate upon the support of the people for the maintenance of their own rights."[58]

Jefferson seemed less concerned about his compact theory of federalism when he pressured the Massachusetts governor to reduce imports of food, dispatched gunboats off the coast of New England to capture smugglers and offered stern advice to the governor of Vermont in dealing with Canadian smugglers: "I think it so important in example to crush these audacious proceedings, and to make the offenders feel the consequences of individuals daring to oppose a law by force, that no effort should be spared to compass the object."[59]

Jefferson spoke in equally harsh terms to those American fortunes built in circumvention of the embargo laws as "the unlawful profits of the most worthless part of society."[60] The president justified his embargo's seeming violations of his principles of decentralized power and economic freedom with appeals to national security and independence; and although this policy became increasingly unpopular, it was retained as the only practicable alternative to war or national humiliation.

In the areas of presidential policy in which Jefferson seemed to abandon his own democratic ideals: the Louisiana Purchase and the embargo, his principal biographers describe these lapses as "pragmatic" adjustments to extreme circumstances and remind us that Jefferson was "less doctrinaire" in office than outside it.[61] Another, less sympathetic, assessment might be that Jefferson, like most men, could succumb to the temptations of power and,

---

[58] Ibid., p. 584.
[59] Ibid., p. 603.
[60] Ibid., p. 591.
[61] Malone, *Jefferson the President, First Term,* p. 332; Peterson, *Thomas Jefferson and the New Nation,* p. 789.

as with his illusions over slavery, he was capable, as president, of enjoying the executive prerogatives that he resisted so effectively when exercised by the Federalists.

CHAPTER 6

ETHICS AND DEMOCRACY

THOMAS JEFFERSON'S conception of a virtuous American republic presumed the existence of a social ethics appropriate to
a naturally social being possessing a divinely ordained moral
sense. This was the religion of Christian ethics, which conformed
to man's natural sympathies and fostered a sense of duty to his
fellow citizens. As Jefferson wrote to Adams:

> If by *religion*, we are to understand *sectarian dogmas*, in which no
> two of them agree, then your exclamation . . . is just, 'that this
> would be the best of all possible worlds, if there were no religion
> in it.' But if the moral precepts, innate in man, and made a part
> of his physical condition, as necessary of a social being, if the
> sublime doctrines . . . taught us by Jesus of Nazareth in which all
> agree, constitute true religion, then, without it, this would be, as
> you again say, 'something not fit to be named, even indeed a Hell.'[1]

---

[1] Jefferson to John Adams, May 5, 1817, *The Adams-Jefferson Letters*, 2 vols.,
ed. Lester J. Cappon (Chapel Hill: University of North Carolina Press, 1959),
2:512. See also Eugene R. Sheridan's introduction to Dickenson Ward Adams,
ed., *Jefferson's Extracts from the Gospels* (Princeton, N.J.: Princeton University
Press, 1983); William D. Gould, "Religious Opinions of Thomas Jefferson,"
Mississippi Valley Historical Review 20 (September 1933); George M. Knoles,
"Religious Ideas of Thomas Jefferson," *Mississippi Valley Historical Review* 30
(September 1943); J. Leslie Hall, "The Religious Opinions of Thomas Jefferson,"
Sewanee Review 21 (April 1913); Charles B. Sanford, *The Religious Life of Thomas
Jefferson* (Charlottesville: University Press of Virginia, 1984); Henry Wilder
Foote, *The Religion of Thomas Jefferson* (Boston: Beacon Press, 1960).

ANCIENT MORALS AND CHRISTIAN ETHICS

The shift in Jefferson's preferences in moral philosophy—from the "heathan moralists" of antiquity to Christian ethics—corresponds with the development in his political theory.[2] The change from the moral precepts found in Homer, Epicurus, and Cicero to those found in Christ, reflected a distinction in Jefferson's mind between morals as purely a private concern (enhancing the individual's "self-realization") and morals as essentially of public concern (enhancing a well ordered, harmonious society). And, as Jefferson considered man's distinguishing characteristic his social nature, derived from the moral sense, he naturally considered that system of ethics which instructed and enhanced man's social nature necessarily superior. Hence, Jefferson increasingly distinguished between ancient moral philosophy and Christian ethics on the basis of the former serving *private* goodness and well being (i.e., one's duties to oneself) and the latter serving *public* goodness and well being (i.e., one's duties to others and to society). Thus, of the classical Greek and Roman moral philosophers[3] Jefferson wrote: "Their precepts relate chiefly to ourselves, and the government of those passions which, unrestrained, would disturb our tranquillity of mind."[4] They include those obligations which man "owes himself, to precepts of rendering him impassable, and unassailable by the evils of life, and for preserving his mind in a state of constant serenity. . . . In this branch of philosophy they were really great."[5]

---

[2]This shift has been noted by several Jefferson scholars, but has not been adequately related to the development of his political philosophy. See Adrienne Koch, *The Philosophy of Thomas Jefferson* (New York: Columbia University Press, 1943), ch. 4; Gilbert Chinard's introduction to Jefferson's *The Literary Bible of Thomas Jefferson* (Baltimore: Johns Hopkins Press, 1928), pp. 18, 35–36; and Sheridan's introduction to Adams, *Jefferson's Extracts from the Gospels.*

[3]Jefferson cites Pythagoras, Socrates, Epicurus, Cicero, Epictetus, Seneca, and Antoninus as the leading ancient moral philosophers (see Jefferson to Dr. Benjamin Rush, April 21, 1803, *The Complete Jefferson,* ed. Saul K. Padover [New York: Tudor, 1943], p. 948).

[4]Ibid.

[5]Jefferson to Adams, Oct. 12, 1813, *A-JL,* 2:384–85. See also Jefferson to William Short, October 31, 1816, *The Writings of Thomas Jefferson,* 20 vols., ed. Albert Ellery Bergh (Washington, D.C.: Memorial ed., 1904–1905), 15:220.

If this were the sum of man—if he were merely a solitary creature capable only of refining his own self-control and personal serenity—the ancient moralists would be enough. But Jefferson regarded man as essentially a social and political being, requiring participation in the human community for his full development and happiness, and therefore in need of an ethical creed which enhances relations among individuals and promotes social harmony.[6] It was into the world of classical self-perfection, insisted Jefferson, that Jesus gave a moral philosophy suited to man's true, God-given nature: "His moral doctrines, relating to kindred and friends were more pure and perfect than those of the most correct of philosophers and . . . went far beyond in inculcating universal philanthropy not only to kindred and friends, to neighbors and countrymen, but to all mankind, gathering all into one family, under the bond of love, charity, peace, common wants and common aids. . . . [Herein lies] the peculiar superiority of the system of Jesus over all others."[7]

Christ's ethical teachings of love, repentence and forgiveness, of universal brotherhood and charity provided, for Jefferson, "the most sublime and benevolent code of morals which has ever been offered to man" for his life in society.[8] "Epictetus and Epicurus gave laws for governing ourselves, Jesus a supplement of the duties and charities we owe to others."[9] But, the Christian Ethics which Jefferson felt suited man's social nature and contributed to America's virtuous republic, were often lost, in his

---

[6] So, Jefferson's criticism of the ancient moral philosophers runs along these lines: "In developing our duties to others, they were short and defective. They embraced, indeed, the circles of kindred and friends, and inculcated patriotism, or the love of our country in the aggregate, as a primary obligation; towards our neighbors and countrymen they taught justice, but scarcely viewed them as within the circle of benevolence. Still less have they inculcated peace, charity, and love of our fellow-men, or embraced with benevolence the whole family of mankind" (Jefferson to Dr. Benjamin Rush, April 21, 1803, *CJ*, p. 948).

John Diggins notes ironically that Jefferson took the relation of Christian ethics to politics much more seriously than his more orthodox brethren (such as John Adams); see Diggins, *The Lost Soul of American Politics* (New York: Basic Books, 1984), p. 79.

[7] Jefferson to Dr. Benjamin Rush, April 21, 1803, *CJ*, p. 949.

[8] Jefferson to John Adams, October 12, 1813, *A-JL*, 2:384.

[9] Jefferson to William Short, October 31, 1819, *WTJ*, 15:220.

opinion, in the elaborate ceremonies, dogmas, and institutions of the various churches.

THE CHURCH AND CHRISTIAN ETHICS

While extolling the ethical teachings of Christ, Jefferson distinguished between the "genuine" lessons of Jesus and the "spurious" dogmas of various disciples and sectarian orders. To separate the true teachings of Christ from their specious imitations (which Jefferson considered as easily distinguishable as "the gold from the dross," the "grain from the chaff," or "as diamonds in a dunghill"),[10] he composed a *Philosophy of Jesus* and a *Life and Morals of Jesus,* by extracting those portions of the Gospels which presented the ethics in their purest, most simple form.[11] Ironically, it was his abiding and reverent belief in these Christian ethical teachings that led Jefferson to criticize the institutionalized church, but which also led many to question his religious sincerity. His specific attacks on the church and clergy (especially the established Anglican church of Virginia in which he was baptized and served as vestryman) reveal his adherence to essential Christian principles. Jefferson repeatedly chastised the church for not living up to its divine mission, for not upholding the purity of the Christian faith in a corrupt world. He attacked the church for neglecting its duties, for its venality and hypocrisy in serving worldly authorities rather than measuring them against the high standards of Christian faith and by preaching poverty, peace, charity, and humility while practicing extravagance, persecution, and self-righteous pride.[12] Indeed, Jefferson's principal complaint against the Church was that its distortions of Christ's ethical teachings, essential to a virtuous republic, drove good people away:

---

[10] Quoted in Koch, *The Philosophy of Thomas Jefferson,* p. 23.

[11] See Adams, *Jefferson's Extracts from the Gospels.*

[12] See Jefferson to John Adams, May 5, 1817, *A-JL,* 2:512; to Wendover, March 13, 1815, *CJ,* pp. 953–55, and to Dr. Benjamin Waterhouse, June 26, 1822, p. 956.

They are mere usurpers of the Christian name, teaching a counter-religion made up of the *deliria* of crazy imaginations as foreign from Christianity as is that of Mahomet. Their blasphemies have driven thinking men into infidelity, who have too hastily rejected the supposed author himself, with the horrors so falsely imputed to him. Had the doctrines of Jesus been preached always as pure as they came from his lips, the whole civilized world would now have been Christian.[13]

Jefferson's remedy for this perversion of true Christian teaching was the establishment of absolute religious freedom in America, from which, he hoped, through the clashing of various denominational interpretations of Christianity, the simple ethical teachings of Christ might be distilled.

FREEDOM OF RELIGION AND CHRISTIAN ETHICS

Religious freedom and toleration, for Jefferson, was to serve the higher purpose of encouraging debate and dialogue among the various denominations, from which the simple ethical teaching of Christ, vital to Jefferson's vision of a virtuous republic, might be distilled and disseminated. As he wrote to Dr. Benjamin Waterhouse, "I rejoice that in this blessed country of free inquiry and belief, which has surrendered its creed and conscience to neither kings nor priests, the genuine doctrine of one God is reviving, and I trust that there is not a *young man* now living in the United States who will not die [a true Christian]."[14] He

---

[13] Jefferson to Dr. Benjamin Waterhouse, ibid. See also Jefferson to John Adams, May 5, 1817, ibid.; and to Peter Carr, August 10, 1787, *WTJ*, 6:258–59.

Of course, along with denouncing church pretensions, Jefferson also, in rather typical Enlightenment fashion, rejected the "metaphysical" doctrines in Christianity (e.g., original sin, Christ's divinity, his immaculate conception, resurrection, etc.); that is, he wished to retain the "practical" aspects of Christian ethics while dismissing the "mystical" aspects of Christian theology.

[14] Jefferson to Dr. Benjamin Waterhouse, ibid. Jefferson's letter ends "die a Unitarian," which for him *was* a true Christian (see Daniel Boorstin, *The Lost World of Thomas Jefferson* [New York: Henry Holt, 1948], p. 156).

hoped that through freedom of religious practice and discussion that those basic teachings of Christ common to all denominations would gain ascendancy, bringing all religious people together and promoting peace and justice in the American republic. In his first inaugural address, Jefferson expressed this hoped-for effect of religious freedom, describing the country as "enlightened by a benign religion, professed, indeed, and practiced in various forms, yet all of them including honesty, truth, temperance, gratitude, and the love of man; acknowledging and adoring an overruling Providence."[15]

Thus, quite the contrary of emanating from a hostility or indifference toward Christianity, Jefferson's advocacy of religious freedom was designed to preserve true Christian teachings from the corruption of worldly institutions: "Had not the Roman government permitted free inquiry Christianity could never have been introduced. Had not free inquiry been indulged at the era of the reformation, the corruptions of Christianity could not have been purged away. If it be restrained now, the present corruptions will be protected, and new ones encouraged."[16]

Jefferson's "Bill for Establishing Religious Freedom" began this process of cleansing the Church by denouncing the established Anglican church for "impiously" obstructing the Christian faith:

Almighty God hath created the mind free . . . all attempts to influence it by temporal punishments, or burthens, or by civil incapacitations, tend only to beget habits of hypocrisy and meanness, and are a departure from the plan of the holy author of our religion. . . . [T]he impious presumption of legislature and ruler, civil as well as ecclesiastical . . . [to] have assumed dominion over the faith of others . . . tends also to corrupt the principle of that very religion it is meant to encourage.[17]

---

[15] Jefferson, "First Inaugural Address," *CJ*, p. 385.

[16] From Jefferson's *Notes on the State of Virginia*, *CJ*, p. 675.

[17] Jefferson, Bill for Establishing Religious Freedom, *CJ*, p. 946. It was in relation to an established state church that Jefferson made his famous reference to the "wall of separation" between church and state to the Connecticut Baptists (though even there he wishes for religious freedom to encourage citizens' "social

But the disestablishment of the Anglican church did not, for Jefferson, automatically result in complete religious freedom (by which he understood the exposure to various denominational creeds, from which the true, simple teachings of Jesus might be distilled). So, for example, Jefferson opposed the establishment of a Chair of Divinity at the University of Virginia not because he wished to exclude religion from that public institution, but because a *single* Chair of Divinity would imply representation of only one denomination (just as had the established church): "It was not, however, to be understood that instruction in religious opinion and duties was meant to be precluded by the public authorities, as indifferent to the interests of society. On the contrary, the relations which exist between man and his Maker, and the duties resulting from those relations, are the most interesting and important to every human being, and the most incumbent on his study and investigation."[18]

Jefferson's solution to the problem of one dominant religious sect in the public university was not to exclude all religion from the institution, but to invite the free expression of *all* denominations within the university's walls.

> A remedy . . . has been suggested of promising aspect, which, while it excludes the public authorities from the domain of religious freedom, will give to the sectarian schools of divinity the full benefit the public provisions made for instruction in the other branches of science. . . . It has, therefore, been in contemplation, and suggested by some pious individuals, who perceive the advantages of

---

duties," i.e., knowledge of Christian ethics):

> I contemplate with sovereign reverence that act of the whole American people which declared that their legislature should "make no law respecting an establishment of religion, or prohibit the free exercise thereof," thus building a wall of separation between church and state. Adhering to this expression of the supreme will of the nation in behalf of the rights of conscience, I shall see with sincere satisfaction the progress of those sentiments which tend to restore to man all his natural rights, convinced he has no natural right in opposition to his social duties. (Letter to A Committee of the Danbury Baptist Association, January 1, 1802, *CJ*, pp. 518–19)

[18] Jefferson, October 7, 1822, *CJ*, p. 957.

associating other studies with those of religion, to establish their
religious schools on the confines of the University, so as to give
their students ready and convenient access and attendance on the
scientific lectures of the University. . . . Such establishments would
offer the further and greater advantage of enabling the students of
the University to attend religious exercises with the professor of
their particular sect, either in the rooms of the building still to be
erected . . . or in the lecturing room of such professor. . . . Such
an arrangement would complete the circle of useful sciences embraced by this institution, and would fill the chasm now existing,
on principles which would leave inviolate the constitutional freedom of religion.[19]

The presence of all religious denominations within the walls of
the public university would give students the opportunity to be
exposed to all dogmas, from which, Jefferson hoped, they might
distill that which was common to them all—the basic ethical
teachings of Jesus—to the benefit of the virtuous American republic, without imposing a single religious creed or violating
their religious freedom.

This understanding of freedom of religion is also revealed in
Jefferson's description of religious life in Charlottesville, where
the absence of church buildings compelled the separate denominations to worship together, taking turns conducting services
in the public courthouse:

In our village of Charlottesville there is a good deal of religion,
with only a small spice of fanaticism. We have four sects, but without
either church or meeting house. The courthouse is the common
temple, one Sunday in the month to each. Here Episcopalian and
Presbyterian, Methodist and Baptist, meet together, join in hymn-
ing their Maker, listen with attention and devotion to each other's
preachers and all mix in society with perfect harmony.[20]

---

[19]Ibid., pp. 957–58.

[20]Jefferson to Dr. Thomas Cooper, November 2, 1822, *WTJ,* 15:404, quoted
in Foote, *The Religion of Thomas Jefferson,* pp. 7–8. Despite this ecumenical
sentiment, Jefferson, two years later, contributed to the building of separate
houses of worship, showing a decided partiality to his own Episcopal church.
His account book of March 8, 1824 reads: "I have subscribed to the building
of an Episcopal church, two hundred dollars; a Presbyterian church, sixty dollars;
and a Baptists, twenty-five dollars" (p. 8).

Such social harmony was precisely what Jefferson hoped freedom of religion would produce in the American republic, as the diverse expression of religious belief distilled the simple ethical teachings of Jesus, fostering love, cooperation, mutual respect, and toleration.[21]

[21] Jefferson's general appreciation of the relation between ethics and politics is revealed in a letter to Judge Augustus B. Woodward (March 24, 1824, *WTJ*, 16:19), in which he states that he regards "ethics, as well as religion, as supplements to law in the government of men"; and to William Johnson (June 1823, *CJ*, p. 322) that "the state's moral rule of their citizens" will be enhanced by its "enforcing moral duties and restraining vice."

CHAPTER 7

THE CULTURE OF
THE VIRGINIA GENTRY AND
THOMAS JEFFERSON, ESQUIRE

WHILE IDEOLOGICALLY Jefferson reflected a constellation of British liberalism, classical republicanism, moral sense philosphy, and Christian ethics, culturally he resided within the world of the landed gentry. Although his membership in that social class seems to have affected his manner, tastes, and style more than his politics, it also had a profound effect on his attitudes toward an institution that challenged his entire political philosophy: slavery.

THE ENGLISH GENTRY
ON VIRGINIAN ESTATES

The gentry class of seventeenth-century England does not fall neatly into most social categories. This is because the English gentry was an intermediate class—economically, politically, and psychologically. The gentry consisted of landed freeholders engaged in market trade. As such, members of the gentry constituted a transitional class, with one foot in a traditional feudal realm and one in the modern world, sharing certain traits with each epoch while never residing entirely in either. Like their counterparts in Virginia, the English gentry often occupied an ambivalent position between the Court and Country values.[1] Although English gentry was not purely a military aristocracy bound by medieval feudal tenure and strict allegiance to the king, it was fervently attached to the land and to a semblance of timocratic codes of honor (now taking the form of "manners") and preserved a mild contempt for commerce, cities, and traders.[2] But neither was the gentry a commercial oligarchy, concerned simply with material gain and the accumulation of wealth (as the growing class of merchants), though it did condescend to engage in trade and soon was heavily dependent on the market economy for both luxuries and its elevated social position.[3] And while the gentry was certainly not democratic (taking freedom and equality as principal tenets of its political creed) its rather tenuous social position between monarchical authority and mercantile wealth rendered it sympathetic to various bourgeois reforms (unrestrained inheritance, extended suffrage, etc.), though it regularly displayed revulsion toward the squalid urban masses which often accompanied such reforms.

A general portrait of the English gentry reveals a complex, transitional class of landed freeholders conducting, in altered form, the feudal nobility's code of honor and attachment to the country and certain of its customs while sharing the merchant's affinity for trade and occasionally aligning itself with the democratic critique of social consequences inherent in both medieval custom and capitalist wealth. Thus the gentry found itself caught between two dominant historical eras, embodying qualities

---

[1] A. G. Roeber, *Faithful Magistrates and Republican Lawyers* (Chapel Hill: University of North Carolina Press, 1981), pp. xvii–xviii, 27.

[2] See J. G. A. Pocock's discussion of "manners" in *Virtue, Commerce, and History* (Cambridge: Cambridge University Press, 1985), p. 49.

[3] Phillip Alexander Bruce, *Economic History of Virginia in the Seventeenth Century* (New York: Macmillan, 1907), p. 1; Thomas J. Wertenbaker, *Patrician and Plebian in Virginia* (New York: Russell & Russell, 1959), pp. ii, 67; Louis B. Wright, *The First Gentlemen of Virginia* (San Marino: Huntington Library, 1940), pp. 26, 47; Charles S. Sydnor, *Gentlemen Freeholders* (Chapel Hill: University of North Carolina Press, 1952); Rhys Isaac, *The Transformation of Virginia, 1740–1790* (Chapel Hill: University of North Carolina Press, 1982), pp. 21–30, 40–42.

which were both unique and destined for extinction.

The country life and manners of the English gentry were consciously replicated in eighteenth-century Virginia.[4] Several influences contributed to this deliberate duplication of English country life: first, the emigration of English aristocrats to Virginia, especially during their persecution under the Puritans;[5] and second, the emigration of younger sons of English nobility who were excluded from landed inheritance by the laws of primogeniture and entail, but who might establish estates in the New World.[6] Both of these groups could naturally and easily set themselves up in country houses in the wilds of Virginia resembling those left behind in England; but perhaps the greater number of such estates were actually built by middle-class elements (merchants, yeomen, professionals) who assimilated into the dominant cultural ideal of the country life and aspired to realize it for themselves and their descendents.[7] After all, even in England at this time, the gentry class was continually replenished by such newly-arrived individuals.[8]

Both the natural and the contrived reconstructions of English country life were reinforced by the gentry culture transported to Virginia. A studied adherence to the forms and manners of landed society—mansion houses, ancestral pretensions, English architecture and gardens, upper-class education and sports (and even

---

[4]Henry Adams, *History of the United States During the Administrations of Jefferson and Madison,* ed. Ernest Samuels (Chicago: University of Chicago Press, 1967), p. 98; Thomas Nelson Page, *The Old Dominion: Her Making and Her Manners* (New York: Scribners', 1908); Philip Alexander Bruce, *Social Life of Virginia in the Seventeenth Century* (Lynchburg: Bell, 1927), pp. vii, 23–25; Wertenbaker, *Patrician and Plebian in Virginia,* p. 25; Wright, *First Gentlemen of Virginia,* pp. 2–4; Joyce Appleby, *Capitalism and a New Social Order* (New York: New York University Press, 1984), p. 7; John Murrin, "The Great Inversion, or Court versus Country," in J. G. A. Pocock, *Three British Revolutions, 1641, 1688, 1776* (Princeton, N.J.: Princeton University Press, 1980), pp. 385, 426.

[5]Bruce, *Social Life of Virginia,* pp. 19, 73.

[6]Ibid., pp. 12, 77; Wertenbaker, *Patrician and Plebian in Virginia,* p. vi; Wright, *First Gentlemen of Virginia,* p. 7.

[7]Bruce, *Economic History of Virginia,* p. 1; Wertenbaker, *Patrician and Plebian in Virginia,* pp. ii–vii; W. J. Cash, *The Mind of the South* (New York: A. A. Knopf, 1941), chs. 1, 3.

[8]Wright, *First Gentlemen of Virginia,* pp. 6–7, 48.

sporting dogs)—were carefully transplanted to Virginian soil and cultivated all the more diligently for their distance from the real thing. As Rhys Isaac illustrates in *The Transformation of Virginia*, however, this traditional gentry culture was fairly shortlived. By the second quarter of the eighteenth century, Virginia had developed a traditional system of social differentiation through law, education, architecture, and ceremony, but "[a]fter 1740 this order, only just settling into its newly built classical mansions, courthouses, and churches of brick began to undergo radical changes."[9] Isaac shows how this traditional hierarchical and authoritarian culture was "hardly consolidated before it began to be subverted."[10] The dignity and order underlying the noble character of the Virginia gentry, represented in the Anglican liturgy reinforcing "an ethos of English Christian gentility," soon was challenged and eventually overrun by the egalitarian and democratic Baptist culture of the majority of poor farmers in the commonwealth.[11] Still, symbols of the traditional culture of the Virginia gentry lingered on, despite its declining social stature and political authority. Perhaps the most telling characteristic of this transplanted gentry culture (and most significant for our understanding of Jefferson) was its enthusiastic regard for a particular standard of social conduct, its self-conscious aspiring toward the English ideal of the "Christian Gentleman."

AN ARISTOCRATIC IDEAL: THE CHRISTIAN GENTLEMAN

In their most perfect form, the life and habits of the gentry were intended to breed a certain kind of gentleman, whose character—in both private and public contact—epitomized that which was best of the various classes from which the gentry was derived. This type of patriarch, friend, and citizen attained a higher development in Virginia than perhaps any other American colony;

---

[9] Isaac, *Transformation of Virginia*, p. 135.
[10] Ibid., p. 141.
[11] Ibid., pp. 60–64, 164–73.

and there, as elsewhere, the ideal of the Christian gentleman implied several distinctive traits.[12]

First, the worldview of this gentleman entailed an organic vision of society, an integral conception of social relations inherited from feudalism. From their superior position within that organic whole, these landed gentlemen received both social privileges and social obligations. The privileges attending their elevated position included a stable and recognized place in society characterized by dignity, wealth, and honor. But gentlemen were not vulgar bourgeois—claiming their privileges from individual enterprise and abstract right; gentlemen acknowledged their dependence on other classes in society and their obligations to the community and especially to the weakest members of it. As Melvin Yazawa explains this temperament in *From Colonies to Commonwealth*, "The familial commonwealth placed a premium on the intricacies of mutual dependence. A 'Mutual good Affection' founded on . . . cheerful obedience on the one hand and judicious discretion on the other."[13] In practical terms, and in striking contrast to modern legalism, this gentleman's appreciation of his place prescribed a general beneficence, along with a revulsion at ever taking advantage of another's misfortunes or reduced circumstances. If anything, the gentleman's code of conduct required deference inverse to another's status: extraordinary kindness and generosity to those of inferior station and mild contempt toward those of power and wealth (especially wealth).[14]

The gentleman's position necessarily required training in leadership appropriate to both his public and private duties.[15] His

---

[12] For contemporaneous works on the English gentleman see Henry Peacham, *The Compleat Gentleman* (1622); Richard Brathwaite, *The English Gentlemen* (1630); *Lord Chesterfield's Letters to His Son* (1774); for an excellent and sympathetic treatment of its Virginian counterpart, see Wright, *First Gentlemen of Virginia*.

[13] Melvyn Yazawa, *From Colonies to Commonwealth: Familial Ideology and the Beginnings of the American Republic* (Baltimore: Johns Hopkins University Press, 1985), p. 141.

[14] Yazawa's *From Colonies to Commonwealth* traces the transformation of this traditional familial model of social relations in America to the postrevolutionary republican legalism, in which the impersonal law becomes "king" (see ch. 6).

[15] Wright, *First Gentlemen of Virginia*, p. 3.

code of manners enhanced that position by combining a classical regard for excellence with a medieval sense of honor and a Christian concern for the poor and meek. The central component of such manners was therefore courtesy: an instinctive regard for others' circumstances and sensibilities combined with the will to accommodate them for the goodness and harmony of the whole, as well as the comfort of oneself. A gentleman's courtesy involved a dignified kindness untainted by ostentation, an easy grace fortified by strength of character, a seemingly natural ability to mix with individuals of every condition and to address their particular needs with sensitivity, authenticity, and humility. Such a code of manners had direct political and personal implications, for they were designed, in both spheres, to promote harmonious and pleasant social relations. This was considered especially important in early encounters: If initial politeness, while admittedly superficial, smoothed over the rough edges of human intercourse, affections might be allowed to develop which would preserve the relations during inevitable conflict in the future. Gentlemanly manners thus acknowledged the fact of human psychology that differences between individuals might be resolved without permanent damage to the relationship if occurring on a base of cultivated deference. As such, the gentleman's code of conduct, so often caricatured, synthesized classical Greek and Christian ethics by at once admiring others' excellences while accepting their weaknesses.[16] The "easy affability of the gentleman" allowed one to be capable of formality when circumstances required and "to disregard convention without transgressing good manners."[17]

The conduct which best blended the gentleman's private do-

---

[16] Jefferson expressed this synthesis in advice to young Peter Carr, emphasizing both Aristotelean generosity and Christian charity, along with the medieval virtue of honor: "lose no occasion of exercising your dispositions to be grateful, to be generous, to be charitable, to be humane, to be true, just, firm, orderly, courageous, etc. Consider every act of this kind as an exercise which will strengthen your moral faculties and increase your worth" (August 10, 1787, *The Writings of Thomas Jefferson*, 20 vols., ed. Albert Ellery Bergh [Washington, D.C., Memorial ed., 1904–1905], 6:258).

[17] Wright, *First Gentlemen of Virginia*, p. 8. Cf. Plato's *Republic*, book 3, 401d–402e; Isaac, *The Transformation of Virginia*, p. 260.

mestic life and his social and political responsibilities was his famous hospitality. Southerners' affinity for "gracious hospitality," when viewed apart from its caricature, served to bring strangers within the familiar affections of family, extending domestic tranquility into social relations outside the home.[18] The gentlemanly quality most congenial to this hospitality was a generous spirit: generosity with both money and time—acknowledging the proper subordination of both to friendly, harmonious social intercourse. This southern trait was noted by a New Englander who described it as "the absence of mercantile sharpness and quickness, the rusticity and open-handed hospitality which could exist only where the struggle for life was hardly a struggle at all."[19] Similar is A. G. Bradley's recollection of Colonel Broomsedge:

> And as he sat upon the porch or with his chair tilted back against his favorite mulberry-tree, he kept his eye fastened on the road. And the traveler who was shouted to by the Colonel to "lite and sit awhile" and could resist that tone of hospitable command, must have been an individual wholly unsuited to dwell upon Virginian soil—some despicable pettifogger who carried a watch about and grudged an hour or two for genial interchange of views on politics, or farming, or the war, much less for a homily on foxhunting.[20]

Of course, as the transformation of Virginian culture from an authoritarian gentry to an egalitarian democracy occurred, the idea that gentlemen's houses were "sacrosanct settings for hospitality" also diminished, so that by the 1780s it was almost nonexistent (except at Thomas Jefferson's Monticello).[21]

The country gentlemens' social position and outlook commended a consistent, if often nominal, adherence to the Christian religion, and in both Britain and Virginia, to the established Anglican church. The blend of "formality and informality of

---

[18]Wright, ibid., p. 31.

[19]In Henry Adams, *History of the United States*, p. 97. The northern visitor also wrote: "they *love money less* than we do; they are more disinterested; their patriotism is not tied to their purse strings" (p. 98).

[20]A. G. Bradley, *Sketches from Old Virginia* (New York: Macmillan, 1897), p. 80.

[21]Isaac, *Transformation of Virginia*, pp. 71, 302.

convivial engagement and structured relationship" in the Church of England's liturgy and hierarchy reinforced the traditionally ordered society and the superior status of the landed gentry.[22] Quoting the description of a typical Virginia Anglican clergyman as "facetious and good-humored, without too much freedom and licentiousness" Rhys Isaac remarked, "Wanted, a parson who can carry his religion, as he should his liquor, like a gentleman!"[23]

Christianity's organic social creed, as discussed earlier, was congenial with the gentry, as was the courage and stoicism inherited from their military progenitors.[24] Consistent with their patriarchal form of governance, the gentleman's attitude toward women, or at least toward ladies, was prescribed by the code of chivalry.[25] A gentleman did not take pleasure in seeing women dig ditches or practice armed combat.

Still, unless one becomes overwhelmed by the noble qualities of this ideal Christian gentleman, it is important to mention the common moral transgressions of this class, transgressions so common as to render them almost obligatory. The two most common excesses of this gentlemanly clan were exorbitant imbibing of alcoholic refreshment and "lack of continency" with respect to certain classes of women.[26] Hence the finest parody on English gentlemen is Shakespeare's Sir John Falstaff, who described himself this way: "I was as virtuously given as a gentleman need to be; virtuous enough; swore little; diced not above seven times a week; went to a bawdy-house not above once in a quarter—of an hour; paid money that I borrowed, three or four times; lived well and in good compass; and now I live out of all order, out of all compass" (*Henry IV,* part 1, act 3, scene 3). Or, as

---

[22] Ibid., pp. 60–64.

[23] Ibid., pp. 120–21.

[24] Wright, *First Gentlemen of Virginia,* pp. 66, 91.

[25] Ibid., p. 84; Wertenbaker, *Patrician and Plebian in Virginia,* p. 66 (cf. "a gentleman, and a Christian," in Cervantes, *Don Quixote,* trans. Peter A. Motteux, (New York: Modern Library, 1930), ch. 2, p. 236).

[26] Wright, *First Gentlemen of Virginia,* pp. 9, 31, 88. As Henry Adams said of his southern friend at Harvard, "Lee was a gentleman of the old school, and, as everyone knows, gentlemen of the old school drank almost as much as gentlemen of the new school" (*The Education of Henry Adams* [Boston: Houghton Mifflin Company, 1918], p. 58).

James Reid, a Scotsman who served as a tutor for a Virginia gentry family wrote, "if a [man] . . . has money, Negroes and Land enough he is a compleat Gentleman. These . . . hide all his defects, usher him into (what they call) the best of company. . . . His madness then passes for wit, his extravagance for flow of spirit, his insolence for bravery, and his cowardise for wisdom."[27]

But even in those common gentlemanly transgressions, Jack Falstaff notwithstanding, one was expected to conduct oneself within standards of discretion and responsibility. Vices were to be exercised in moderation, so as not to inordinately interfere with those duties and accomplishments attending one's station. Among those activities were dancing, riding, and music which, after Plato's education, served as training for courage, decency, fair-play, harmony, and balance—all necessary to the gentleman's ruling character.[28]

Likewise, the gentleman was expected to possess an uncommon degree of knowledge, deriving from an education emphasizing breadth over depth (the classics, humanities, natural science, etc.), implying an understanding not merely of separate facts but of the relations among phenomena—a form of understanding appropriate to men charged with governing a whole community, and acknowledging the fact that political wisdom encompasses philosophy, psychology, history, economics, and ethics. This country gentleman qua Renaissance man was reflected in the several great libraries of notable Virginians, which themselves symbolized less an Enlightenment thirst for knowledge with which to manipulate and control nature as much as a traditional aristocratic need for knowledge of the whole in which one is an active and responsible part.[29]

And while the gentry was continually replenished by pros-

---

[27] Quoted in Isaac, *Transformation of Virginia*, p. 118.

[28] Wright, *First Gentlemen of Virginia*, pp. 10–11; Wertenbaker, *Patrician and Plebian in Virginia*, pp. iii, 73, 105–7. Cf. Plato's discussion of educating ruling philosophical souls through harmony in music and courage in athletics (*The Republic*, book 3, 413d–414a, book 4, 486d–487b).

[29] See Richard Beale Davis, *Intellectual Life in Jefferson's Virginia* (Chapel Hill: University of North Carolina Press, 1964); Isaac, *Transformation of Virginia*, p. 51.

perous members of the middle class, who acquired the means to establish themselves in country estates, the gentleman's code of conduct quickly imposed its imperatives on their economic behavior. A Christian gentleman's quality required much more than mere money. His connection with commerce was explicit but removed; trade properly served as a means to more noble ends; and any overly enthusiastic attachment to money or money-making was regarded as a vulgar and unfortunate form of slavery.[30] As is still the case, a sudden acquisition of wealth did not automatically produce gentlemanly manners or a sense of one's social responsibilities; indeed, without the proper education, sudden wealth was likely to produce just the opposite.

Of course, the premier requisite of gentlemanly character and conduct was a certain amount of leisure, leisure with which to cultivate one's mind and manners and social graces and political expertise. In colonial Virginia, bordering a vast virgin wilderness, this plantation leisure was necessarily purchased with slavery. When the reality of an open frontier allowed even indentured servants to escape to farmland of their own, an enslaved working class of identifiable color became the convenient means of replicating English country life in the New World.[31]

THOMAS JEFFERSON, ESQUIRE

Thomas Jefferson remains an exemplar of the gentry class and of the consummate gentleman.[32] The influence of Virginian cul-

---

[30]Wright, *First Gentlemen of Virginia*, p. 26; Bruce, *Economic History of Virginia*, p. 1; Wertenbaker, *Patrician and Plebian in Virginia*, pp. ii, 3, 67. Leo Marx, *The Machine in the Garden* (New York: Oxford University Press, 1964) explains that they had an "aloof attitude" toward acquisitive behavior. Isaac, *Transformation of Virginia*, p. 118.

[31]Wright, *First Gentlemen of Virginia*, p. 45; Wertenbaker, *Patrician and Plebian in Virginia*, p. 145; Dan Lacy, *The White Use of Blacks in America* (New York: McGraw-Hill, 1973), ch. 1; Bertram Wyatt-Brown, *Southern Honor* (New York: Oxford University Press, 1986), chs. 14–16.

[32]"His character could not be denied elevation, versatility, breadth, insight, and delicacy. . . . His tastes were for that day excessively refined. His instincts were those of a liberal European nobleman. . . . He shrank from whatever was rough or coarse, and his yearning for sympathy was almost feminine" (Henry Adams, *History of the United States*, pp. 105–7).

ture on Jefferson was most evident in his personal demeanor, but it also extended generally to his conception of society and political life.

Attached to the land from birth, Jefferson remained close — in spirit if not always in person — to the Virginia countryside. He inherited more than 5,000 acres from his father and acquired another 6,000 by marriage, making him one of the wealthiest landholders in the commonwealth by the time he reached his early thirties.[33] Likewise, Jefferson displayed an aristocratic pride in his paternal ancestry, both as residents of the highest summit in Britain and as an "old family" of Virginia.[34] Colonel Jefferson tied the history of Virginia permanently to his family name by preparing the first map of its territory, symbolically creating its boundaries and expanse. And Jefferson was not yet so far removed from the aristocratic code of honor that he could not include it as quite literally the last word of the Declaration of Independence.[35] When Jefferson finally met George III personally, his complaint over the king's conduct was not that it was "tyrannical" or "usurpatious," but that it was "ungracious"; Mr. Jefferson faulted the King of England for not being a gentleman.[36]

Yet, to these aristocratic tendencies Jefferson added the characteristic gentry involvement in trade, principally tobacco; and his fortunes were increasingly tied to (and eventually ruined by) the market economy.[37] But his gentleman's objections to the trappings of commerce were softened by the presence, in Virginia, of numerous rivers which permitted highly developed market relations without the attending cities, highways, and urban masses.[38] And despite Jefferson's aristocratic and commercial in-

---

[33] Jefferson, *Autobiography of Thomas Jefferson* (Englewood Cliffs, N.J.: Prentice Hall, 1963), p. 21; Merrill Peterson, *Thomas Jefferson and the New Nation* (New York: Oxford University Press, 1970), pp. 9, 28.

[34] Jefferson, *Autobiography*, p. 19.

[35] Ibid., pp. 20, 41.

[36] Ibid., p. 75.

[37] Peterson, *Thomas Jefferson and the New Nation*, pp. 20–28, 923–24, 1007–08.

[38] Thomas Jefferson, *Notes on the State of Virginia*, *The Complete Jefferson*, ed.

terests, he was also democratic enough to author laws abolishing the landed oligarch's traditional protections in primogeniture and entail, and to propose a state constitution which contained provisions granting fifty acres to every citizen; though, as has been shown, Jefferson was not so egalitarian as to renounce entirely all notions of a ruling aristocracy.[39]

Jefferson's personal manner and general political orientation corresponded so closely to the gentleman's code as to render him almost the best living embodiment of its ideal. He dutifully accepted both the privileges and the obligations of his station, showing "the scrupulous fidelity with which he discharged the duties of every relation in life,"[40] using inherited wealth to build an exquisite mansion house in which to raise a large family and display his manifold talents, but always occupying the numerous public offices expected of him by his peers.[41]

Jefferson's own courteous deportment and gentlemanly manner soon became legendary. He himself attributed this accomplished style to training received in the company of a small circle of scholars and friends at William and Mary College. The man principally responsible for Jefferson's training as a young gentleman was also his leading intellectual mentor, Dr. William Small, himself a man of "correct and gentlemanly manners."[42] The happy result of this cultivation of civility on Jefferson's natural capacities was an ease of manner and a graciousness of style that captivated all those whom he encountered.

The Boston Brahmin George Ticknor found Jefferson dignified in appearance and displaying an "ease and graciousness in his manners," while the Englishman Francis Hall was engaged

---

Saul K. Padover (New York: Tudor, 1943), p. 641; this allowed Jefferson to boast that "trade is brought generally to our doors."

[39]Thomas Jefferson, The Bill to Abolish Entails (1776), *CJ*, pp. 88–89; and "Proposed Constitution for Virginia" (1776), p. 109.

[40]Sarah N. Randolph, *The Domestic Life of Thomas Jefferson* (Cambridge, Mass.: University Press, 1939), p. vii.

[41]E. G. Virginia House of Burgesses, Virginia Delegation to the Continental Congress; Virginia Governor, etc; see *Autobiography* and advice to Peter Carr, *WTJ*, 6:262.

[42]Jefferson, *Autobiography*, p. 20.

by "the most gentlemanly and philosophical" conversation when in the presence of his Virginia host.[43] Indeed, it was only their manners and civility that Jefferson considered appropriate for Americans to adopt from their European cousins: "I would wish my countrymen to adopt just so much of European politeness, as to be ready to make all those little sacrifices of self, which render European manners amiable, and relieve society from the disagreeable scenes to which rudeness often subjects it."[44]

Jefferson's own conduct is perhaps best revealed in two anecdotes relayed by his grandson, Colonel Jefferson Randolph:

> His manners were of that polished school of the Colonial Government, so remarkable in its day—under no circumstances violating any of those minor conventional observances which constitute the well-bred gentleman, courteous and considerate to all persons.
>
> On riding out with him when a lad, we met a negro who bowed to us; he returned his bow; I did not. Turning to me, he asked, 'Do you permit a negro to be more of a gentleman than yourself?'
>
> His countenance was mild and benignant, and attractive to strangers. While President, returning on horseback from Charlottesville with company whom he had invited to dinner, and who were, all but one or two, riding ahead of him, on reaching a stream over which there was no bridge, a man asked him to take him up behind and carry him over. The gentleman in the rear coming up just as Mr. Jefferson had put him down and ridden on, asked the man how it happened that he had permitted the others to pass without asking them? He replied: 'From their looks, I did not like to ask them; the old gentleman looked as if he would do it, and I asked him.' He was very much surprised to hear that he had ridden behind the President of the United States.[45]

Likewise, Jefferson's hospitality was freely extended to both friend and stranger and was of such generous proportions as to nearly ruin him financially.[46] Still, he insisted that to truly know

---

[43] In Adrienne Koch, ed., *Jefferson: Great Lives Observed Series* (Englewood Cliffs, N.J.: Prentice-Hall, 1971), pp. 91–93.

[44] Jefferson to Charles Bellini, September 30, 1785, *WTJ*, 5:151–55.

[45] Randolph, *The Domestic Life of Thomas Jefferson*, p. 337.

[46] Peterson, *Thomas Jefferson and the New Nation*, ch. 11; indeed, one of Jefferson's principal criticisms of the Federalists' Alien and Sedition Acts was their

Virginia, one "must travel through the country and accept the hospitality of the country gentlemen."[47] Jefferson once described the secret ingredient of southern hospitality: "our practice of placing our guests at ease, by showing them we are so ourselves, [also allows us to] follow our necessary vocations, in stead of fatiguing them by hanging unremittingly on their shoulders."[48]

Jefferson reserved a deep regard for the Christian religion, after the manner of most Virginia gentlemen. His discountenance over the established Anglican church, as discussed above, did not disturb his adherence to the Christian faith or his abiding conviction that religious ethics are a necessary component of the just polity.

Jefferson's belief in the chivalrous treatment of women went so far as identifying that code with civilization itself. Commenting on the American Indians' practice of forcing their women to perform hard manual labor, Jefferson wrote: "This, I believe is the case with every barbarous people . . . force is law. The stronger sex imposes on the weaker. It is civilization alone which replaces women in the enjoyment of their natural equality. That first teaches us to subdue the selfish passions, and to respect those rights in others which we value in ourselves."[49] But Jefferson's chivalrous regard for women is perhaps best revealed in the response of a young Washington lady charmed by his solicitations: "this man so meek and mild, yet dignified in his manners, with a voice so soft and low, with a countenance so benignant and intelligent . . . put me perfectly at ease [and] at once unlocked my heart."[50]

Admittedly, Jefferson unlocked more than some women's

---

violation of our "national hospitality" (Jefferson, The Kentucky Resolutions, *CJ*, p. 133).

[47] Jefferson to Madame de Staël-Holstein, July 16, 1807, *WTJ*, 9:283.

[48] Jefferson to Francis W. Gilmer, June 7, 1816, *WTJ*, 15:23–27.

[49] Jefferson, *Notes on the State of Virginia*, p. 607. Jefferson's attitude toward women was characterized by the view that they were superior in virtue to men: "Women are formed by nature for attentions, not for hard labor. A woman never forgets one of the numerous train of little offices which belong to her. A man forgets often" ("Travels in France," 1787).

[50] Recorded in Margaret Bayard Smith's *The First Forty Years of Washington Society* (1906), reprinted in Koch, *Jefferson*, pp. 97–99.

hearts; he subscribed to the common transgressions of his class by conducting affairs with married ladies and by keeping a black mistress.[51] All of these affairs were, characteristically, conducted with great discretion, which has made it quite a challenge to either confirm or deny their existence conclusively. A lot of ink has been spilled by loyal Jeffersonians rushing to protect the honor of their hero, most of whom fail to realize that Jefferson might be more offended by their efforts than by the charges. Among the southern gentry such transgressions were not at all uncommon; what was uncommon was the vulgar habit of northern journalists publishing such affairs, and the equally indiscreet habit of well intentioned defenders dignifying such slanders with argument.

With respect to the other favorite vice of gentlemen, Jefferson always preferred French wine to Irish whiskey, and spared no expense in filling a fine cellar. And while visitors to Monticello confirm Jefferson's affinity for vast quantities of wine and punch, they remind us that he always held his liquor "like a gentleman."[52] In manners generally, Jefferson preached what he practiced, providing his code of conduct in letters of advice and instruction to various young wards. He told his grandson that "good humor" preserves "our peace and tranquillity" and "politeness is artificial good humor":[53] "The practice of sacrificing to those whom we meet in society, all the little conveniences and preferences which will gratify them, and deprive us of nothing worth a moment's consideration; it is giving a pleasing and flattering turn to our expressions, which will conciliate others, and make them pleased with us as well as ourselves. How cheap a price for the good will of another!"[54] If only everybody was so accomplished, Jefferson surely thought, how smooth and pleasant all human intercourse might be.

---

[51] With Mrs. Walker and Maria Cosway, and the now famous "Black Sally" Hemings; see Dumas Malone, *Jefferson and His Time*, 6 vols., *Jefferson The Virginian* (Boston: Little, Brown, 1948), 1:448–49; and Fawn Brodie, *Thomas Jefferson: An Intimate History* (New York: Norton, 1975), pp. 54, 76–85.

[52] Jefferson complained in a letter of whiskey's "loathsome effects" while complimenting the salubrious ones of wine and beer (to William Crawford, January 5, 1818, *WTJ*, 19:252).

[53] Jefferson to Thomas Jefferson Randolph, November 24, 1808, *CJ*, p. 1030.

[54] Ibid., p. 1031; and to T. J. Smith, February 21, 1825, p. 1039.

Jefferson gladly participated in the compulsory accomplishments of the Christian gentleman. He exhibited unusual taste in art and music, and uncommon skills in dance and riding. His universal knowledge is well known; it conformed to the gentlemanly standard of knowing something about everything, and was derived from a library whose catalogue encompassed all fields of inquiry.[55]

Finally, Jefferson possessed the correct attitude toward money. He regarded money as a necessary means to higher ends, and made sure that the acquisition of wealth did not compromise its purposes. Born into property, Jefferson was content to maintain a respectable distance from the sordid practices of money-makers. But the market economy that subjected so many of his countrymen to humiliation eventually destroyed his own estate and subjected his descendants to cruel poverty. The fact that his own noble leisure was purchased with the labor of slaves increased Jefferson's ambivalence toward that institution. Unlike most slaveholders, Jefferson saw that the very system which provided leisure for genteel refinements also inevitably corrupted them:

> The whole commerce between master and slave is a perpetual exercise of the most boisterous passions, the most unremitting despotism on the one part, and degrading submission on the other. Our children see this, and learn to imitate it. . . . The parent storms, the child looks on, catches the lineaments of wrath, puts on the same airs in the circle of smaller slaves, gives a loose to the worst of passions, and thus is nursed and educated, and daily exercised in tyranny. . . . The man must be a prodigy who can retain his manners and morals undepraved by such circumstances.[56]

But when he looked at the economic system which was rapidly replacing slavery, that capitalist market which did not merely subject people to others' "worst passions" but all to the nameless

---

[55] See Jefferson's Library Classification, *CJ*, pp. 1070, 1091; his plan for an educational system, pp. 1064–69; his plan for an education of a lawyer, pp. 1043–47; for a young gentleman, pp. 1056–60; on his own library generally, Charles B. Sanford, *Thomas Jefferson and His Library* (Hamden, Conn.: Archon, 1977).

[56] Jefferson, *Notes on the State of Virginia*, p. 676. Cf. Hegel's "Master-Slave Dialectic," in *The Phenomenology of Mind*, trans. J. B. Baillie (New York: Harper & Row, 1967), section B, ch. 4.

forces of supply and demand, Jefferson wondered whether the alternative to slavery really constituted progress. His comparison of working-class existence under British capitalism left him with little optimism for the future:

> In the class of laborers I do not mean to withhold from the comparison that portion whose color has condemned them, in certain parts of our Union, to a subjection to the will of others. Even these are better fed in the States, warmer clothed, and labor less than the journeymen or day laborers of England. They have the comfort, too, of numerous families, in the midst of whom they live without want, or fear of it; a solace that few of the laborers of England possess. They are subject, it is true, to bodily coersion; but are not the hundreds of thousands of British soldiers and seamen subject to the same, without seeing, at the end of their career, when age and accident shall have rendered them unequal to labor, the certainty, which the other has, that he will never want? And has not the British seaman, as much as the African, been reduced to the bondage by force, in flagrant violation of his own consent and of his natural right in his own person?
>
> And with the laborers of England generally, does not the moral coersion of want subject their will as despotically to that of their employer, as the physical constraint does the soldier, the seaman or the slave? . . . I am not advocating slavery. I am not justifying the wrongs we have committed. . . . there is nothing I would not sacrifice to a practicable plan for abolishing every vestige of this moral and political depravity. But I am, at present, comparing the condition and degree of suffering to which oppression has reduced the man of one color, with . . . the man of another color; equally condemning both.[57]

Jefferson's place within the culture of the Virginia gentry, combined with the enlightened and republican qualities of his thought, may explain the painful inconsistencies he expressed over the institution of slavery, which cast a dark shadow over his political philosophy.

---

[57] Jefferson to Thomas Cooper, September 10, 1814, *WTJ*, 14:183–84.

CHAPTER 8

THE SHADOW OF SLAVERY
OVER JEFFERSON'S POLITICAL
PHILOSOPHY

THOMAS JEFFERSON'S views on slavery were colored by the prejudices of the gentry class and shaped by his general political philosophy. Although he regarded the institution of slavery in America as a "hideous evil," Jefferson was ambivalent over the exact status of blacks within the human community. When he saw his ideal classical republic threatened by limitations on the expansion of slavery, he joined the extreme anti-abolitionists in advocating the extension of slavery into the West.[1]

HUMAN NATURE AND AFRICAN SLAVES

The only way that Jefferson could reasonably reconcile slavery with his claim that "all men are created equal" and his ideal polity of independent, educated, and active citizens was to question the equal human status of blacks and whites. In his *Notes on the State of Virginia,* Jefferson cited the popular "scientific" eighteenth-century evidence that blacks were a distinct race between

---

[1]John Chester Miller, *The Wolf by the Ears: Thomas Jefferson and Slavery* (New York: The Free Press, 1977), pp. 2–3.

apes and men, and he based their inferior status on the deficiencies in the human faculties of reason and imagination.[2]

> Comparing them by their faculties of memory, reason, and imagination, it appears to me that in memory they are equal to the whites: in reason much inferior, as I think one could scarcely be found capable of tracing and comprehending the investigations of Euclid; and that in imagination they are dull, tasteless, and anomalous.
>
> His imagination is wild and extravagant, escapes incessantly from every restraint of reason and taste, and in the course of its vagaries, leaves a tract of thought as incoherent and eccentric, as is the course of a meteor through the sky. His subjects should often have led him to a process of sober reasoning; yet we find him always substituting sentiment for demonstration.
>
> I advance it, therefore, as a suspicion only, that the blacks, whether originally a distinct race, or made distinct by time and circumstances, are inferior to the whites in the endowments both of body and mind.[3]

These deficiencies of human reason and imagination (or the capacity for "reflection"), caused black slaves to frequently sleep when not engaged in physical activity, as did most animals: "In general, their existence appears to participate more of sensation than reflection. To this must be ascribed their disposition to sleep when abstracted from their diversions, and unemployed in labor. An animal whose body is at rest, and who does not reflect, must be disposed to sleep of course."[4]

It apparently did not occur to him that the slaves' propensity to sleep might be attributed to their excessive labor in the heat and humidity of central Virginia. Still, in addition to their intellectual deficiencies, Jefferson ascribed blacks' inferiority to their physical differences in color and form.

> And is this difference of no importance? Is it not the foundation of a greater or less share of beauty in the two races? Are not the

---

[2]Ibid., p. 54.

[3]Thomas Jefferson, *Notes on the State of Virginia*, *The Writings of Thomas Jefferson*, 20 vols., ed. Albert Ellery Bergh (Washington, D.C.: Thomas Jefferson Memorial Assoc., 1904–05), 8:382–86.

[4]Ibid., p. 382.

fine mixtures of red and white, the expression of every passion by greater or less suffusions of color in the one, preferable to that external monotony, which reigns in the countenances, that immovable veil of black which covers all the emotions of the other race? Add to these, flowing hair, a more elegant symmetry of form, their own judgment in favor of the whites, declared by their preference of them, as uniformly as is the preference of the Oranootan for the black woman over those of his own species. The circumstance of superior beauty is thought worthy of attention in the propagation of our horses, dogs, and other domestic animals; why not in that of man? Besides those of color, figure, and hair, there are other physical distinctions proving a difference of race. They have less hair on the face and body. They secrete less by the kidneys, and more by the glands of the skin, which gives them a very strong and disagreeable odor.[5]

And although Jefferson praised blacks' superiority in appreciation of musical rhythm, he disparaged their capacity for writing music or the composition of complex harmonies: "In music they are more generally gifted than the whites, with accurate ears for tune and time, and they have been found capable of imaging a small catch. Whether they will be equal to the composition of a more extensive run of melody, or of complicated harmony, is yet to be proved."[6]

Similarly, Jefferson claimed that blacks exhibited bravery in battle, but attributed this more to lack of reasoned forethought toward the dangers of warfare than to genuine military courage: "They are at least as brave, and more adventuresome. But this may proceed from a want of forethought, which prevents their seeing a danger till it be present. When present, they do not go through it with more coolness or steadiness than the whites."[7] For this reason, as well as his nervousness over giving guns to large numbers of Virginia slaves, Jefferson opposed a plan to enlist blacks into the revolutionary army.[8]

Still, despite their propensity to steal (which, again, Jefferson did not connect to their lack of property ownership), Jefferson

---

[5]Ibid., p. 381.
[6]Ibid., p. 383.
[7]Ibid., p. 381.
[8]Miller, *The Wolf by the Ears,* p. 24.

did not deny the human moral sense to blacks, as he observed the virtues of benevolence, integrity, and loyalty in their conduct: "Notwithstanding these considerations which must weaken their respect for the laws of property, we find among them numerous instances of the most rigid integrity, and as many as among their better instructed masters, of benevolence, gratitude, and un-shaken fidelity."[9]

However, when comparing American black slaves with the white slaves of Greek and Roman antiquity, Jefferson found the ancient slaves excelling in art and science, lending support to his argument that the blacks' inferiority was attributable to their native abilities rather than to their enslaved condition.

> Yet notwithstanding these and other discouraging circumstances among the Romans, their slaves were often their rarest artists. They excelled, too, in science, insomuch as to be usually employed as tutors to their masters' children. Epictetus, Terence, and Phoedrus, were slaves. But they were of the race of whites. It is not their condition then, but nature which has produced the distinction.[10]

Still, despite his belief that blacks were inherently inferior to whites, and possibly even a distinct race separate from humans, Jefferson expressed "doubts" over the common attitude of the gentry and even hoped that after several years of liberation from the oppressive bonds of slavery, the blacks might prove themselves equal to whites in all human abilities.

> Be assured that no person living wishes more sincerely than I do, to see a complete refutation of the doubts I have myself entertained and expressed on the grade of understanding allotted to the negroes by nature, and to find that in this respect they are on a par with ourselves. My doubts were the result of personal observation on the limited sphere of my own States, where the opportunities for the development of their genius were not favorable, and those of exercising it still less so.[11]
>
> Nobody wishes more than I do to see such proofs as you exhibit,

---

[9] Jefferson, *Notes on the State of Virginia*, p. 386.
[10] Ibid., p. 384.
[11] Jefferson to Henri Gregoire (1809), *WTJ*, 5:429.

that nature has given to our black brethren talents equal to those of the other colors of men, and that the appearance of a want of them is owing merely to the degraded condition of their existence, both in Africa and America.[12]

I have supposed the black man, in his present state, might not be in body and mind equal to the white man; but it would be hazardous to affirm, that, equally cultivated for a few generations, he would not become so.[13]

Whether or not the future freed black slaves would show themselves to be equal in human abilities with whites, Jefferson consistently denounced the institution of slavery, calling it an "abominable crime," a "political and moral evil," and a "hideous blot" on the American republic, prompted by "avarice and evil."[14]

My sentiments on the subject of slavery of negroes have long since been in possession of the public, and time has only served to give them stronger root. The love of justice and the love of country plead equally the cause of these people, and it is a moral reproach to us that they should have pleaded it so long in vain, and should have produced not a single effort, nay I fear not much serious willingness to relieve them and ourselves from our present condition of moral and political reprobation.[15]

You know that nobody wishes more ardently to see an abolition, not only of the trade, but of the condition of slavery; and certainly nobody will be more willing to encounter every sacrifice for that object.[16]

But, except for a brief period in 1788–1789, Jefferson believed that the abolition of slavery must include the removal and re-settlement of blacks in Africa. As he wrote to Dr. Thomas Humphreys in 1817, "I concur entirely in your leading principles of gradual emancipation, of establishment on the coast of Africa, and the patronage of our nation until the emigrants shall be able

[12]Jefferson to Benjamin Benneker (1791), *WTJ*, 3:291.
[13]Jefferson to General Chastellux (1785), *WTJ*, 1:341.
[14]Jefferson to M. DeMeunier (1786), *WTJ*, 276; *Notes on the State of Virginia*, 8:334; to William Short (1823), *WTJ* 7:310; to Dr. Price (1785), *WTJ*, 1:377.
[15]Jefferson to Edward Coles (1814), *WTJ*, ed. Paul L. Ford, (New York: G. P. Putnam's Sons, 1897), 9:477.
[16]Jefferson to J. P. Brissot DeWarville (1788), ibid., 5:66.

to protect themselves."[17] The reason for his insistence on deportation of ex-slaves (except for that brief period during the beginning of the French Revolution, when he believed they might become "good citizens")[18] was the inherent racial prejudice in both whites and blacks which would continue to foment conflicts between the two groups for generations to come.

> It will probably be asked, why not retain and incorporate the blacks into the State, and thus save the expense of supplying the importation of white settlers, the vacancies they will leave? Deep rooted prejudices entertained by the whites; ten thousand recollections, by the blacks, of the injuries they have sustained; new provocations; the real distinctions which nature has made; and many other circumstances will divide us into parties, and produce convulsions, which will probably never end but in the extermination of the one or the other race.[19]

The freeing and deportation of slaves should follow a slow and orderly emancipation, since the sudden liberation of people in bondage would be tantamount to "abandoning children" (an argument Jefferson used for justifying his own failure to release his personal slaves).[20] Until such time that this gradual emancipation became "practicable," Jefferson urged the kind treatment of slaves, expressing the view that "until more can be done for them, we should endeavor, with those whom fortune has thrown on our hands, to feed and clothe them well, protect them from ill usage, require such reasonable labor as is performed voluntarily by freemen, and be led by no repugnances to abdicate them, and our duties to them. The laws do not permit us to turn them loose, if that were for their good; and to commute them for other property is to commit them to those whose usage of them we cannot control."[21] But for Jefferson, that time became less and less "practicable," as the slavery issue, in his view, became interwoven with the protection of his ideal republic.

---

[17] Jefferson to Dr. Thomas Humphries, *WTJ* (mem. ed.), 7:57.
[18] Miller, *The Wolf by the Ears*, p. 101.
[19] *Notes on the State of Virginia*, 8:380.
[20] Jefferson to Dr. Edward Bancroft (1789), *WTJ* (Ford ed.), 5:66.
[21] Jefferson to Edward Coles (1814), ibid., 9:479.

SLAVERY AND THE PRESERVATION
OF THE REPUBLIC

In Jefferson's draft ordinance of 1784, the new western territories were to be closed to slavery, limiting its expansion in the American republic and encouraging its settlement by the economically independent, participatory citizens necessary to Jefferson's ideal polity. That provision to limit the geographical expansion of slavery lost in Congress by one vote, to Jefferson's dismay.[22] Yet by 1820, and the Missouri Compromise controversy, Jefferson opposed attempts to limit slavery in the western territories, for the same reasons he earlier desired limitation on the institution of slavery: the preservation of his ideal republic against northern financial corruption and political "consolidation."[23] Changes in his own Republican party in the early 1800s and the implicit threat to southern influence in Congress (and thereby republican virtue) caused by the creation of additional nonslave states in the union prompted this change in Jefferson's attitude.

By 1817, the Jeffersonian Republicans, in Jefferson's view, had "out-Federalized" the Federalists by restoring nearly all the old corrupt Federalist policies of the 1790s: the National Bank, protective tariffs favoring northern manufactures, an expanded army and navy for imperial adventures and centralized authority in Washington over domestic, state concerns.[24] Combined with Marshall's "consolidationist" Supreme Court, Jefferson perceived the return of corrupt Hamiltonian intrigue and attempts to reduce the independent republican citizenry to poverty and submission. His Lockean liberal attacks on national power in defense of the decentralized republican states and localities affected his attitudes toward the growing controversy over expansion of slavery into the new western territories.

By virtue of the three-fifths compromise in the United States Constitution, whereby slaves were counted as three-fifths of white citizens for purposes of congressional representation and

---

[22] Miller, *The Wolf by the Ears*, p. 27.
[23] Ibid., p. 226.
[24] Ibid., p. 210.

the electoral college, the South enjoyed a unique advantage in the House of Representatives relative to the nonslave North.[25] By 1820, this allowed the southern states to enjoy twenty congressional representatives above those justified by their white populations. The northern states regarded this political consequence of slavery as very unfair and undemocratic. This caused many Federalists to describe Jefferson as the "Negro President," when those disproportionate representatives in the electoral college allowed him to win the presidential election of 1800.[26] Such northern resentment over the southern states' unfair advantage in Congress fueled the abolitionist movement and the resistance to slavery's expansion into the western territories. In Jefferson's view, however, even the three-fifths rule and the unjust advantage it gave the southern slave-holding states were justified in preserving the classical republic of his dreams. And that included sacrificing the limitation on the expansion of slavery into the West to preserve the republican influence in Congress.[27] If Thomas Jefferson had to choose between earlier elimination of slavery through controls on its geographical expansion and the continued power of the republican South in the national legislature, he had little difficulty in choosing the latter.

In 1819, the U.S. Senate was evenly divided between eleven slave states and eleven free states. The northern states, even with the disadvantage of the three-fifths rule, held a majority in the House of Representatives, making the balance of power in the Senate crucial to the South. When Missouri applied for statehood in 1819 as a slave state that balance could be easily maintained by the equal admission of Maine as a free state. The problem with admitting Missouri, however, was its geographical situation above the Mason-Dixon line, traditionally dividing slave-South and free-North.[28]

Jefferson's support of the admission of Missouri as a slave state, despite this expansion of the institution of slavery to the North and contrary to his earlier objections to expansion of

---

[25] Ibid., pp. 221–22.
[26] Ibid., p. 222.
[27] Ibid., p. 223.
[28] Ibid., p. 224.

slavery westward, revealed his preference for preserving the southern republican regime at any cost. Jefferson's attitudes toward the continuation and expansion of slavery thus always remained subordinate to his ideal political philosophy of an economically independent, active citizenry preserving a virtuous republic. In the 1780s that ideal republic of independent yeoman citizens was best served by a free West; but by the 1820s, with the republican South fighting for survival against the corrupt northern financial interests in Congress, it was best served by a slaveholding West: both North and South.[29] Jefferson still claimed to be in favor of the ultimate elimination of slavery, but as John Chester Miller put it: for Jefferson, "if any action were taken against slavery, it must be by Virginia gentlemen, not by outsiders, and, above all, not by a northern majority acting through Congress."[30]

Jefferson's continued claims to be in favor of black emancipation while resisting the limitations on slavery into the western territories (and his continual questioning of blacks' innate equality with whites) struck many as disingenuous and indefensible. In his own Virginia, his position was not widely accepted. Rather, that of his colleague John Taylor of Caroline County was more popular with Virginian slaveholders and southern Republicans.[31] John Taylor (1753–1824) held that slavery was an unavoidable evil to agrarian, republican America, and that the proper stance toward it was the humane and efficient management of slaves and the strict control of free blacks and mulattoes. Taylor advised providing comfortable clothes, good food, and sturdy houses for the slaves, which would bind the blacks' loyalty to their masters better than chains.[32] But he feared the continual "excitement to insurrection" that free blacks provided for slaves and encouraged strict controls on their movement in the South. Allowing mulattoes to roam freely among black slaves, for Taylor, was "the

---

[29] Ibid., p. 232.
[30] Ibid.
[31] Ibid., p. 262.
[32] John Taylor, *Arator* (1814), ed. M. E. Bradford (Indianapolis: Liberty Classics, 1977), p. 185. Garrett Ward Sheldon, *The Political Thought of John Taylor* (Lawrence: University Press of Kansas, forthcoming, 1992), ch. 4.

policy which first doomed the whites, and then the mulattoes themselves, to the fate suffered by both in St. Domingo" (where slaves freed by the revolutionary French massacred the nonblack population).[33] The solution that Taylor proposed—strict policing of southern slaves and the resettlement in Africa of all freed blacks and mulattoes—was more acceptable to most Virginia slaveholders than Jefferson's plan for gradual, general emancipation. Still, Taylor agreed with Jefferson that slavery was "a misfortune to agriculture" and the sturdy yeoman republican citizen, and he hoped for its eventual demise by economic means.[34]

Thomas Jefferson long hoped that the unprofitability of slavery, so evident in the ruined plantations of eastern Virginia, would cause the eventual demise of the institution, replacing it with more efficient free white farmers using scientific techniques, regardless of the social or political ramifications of slavery. His hope was disappointed by the early 1800s, when, with Eli Whitney's invention of the cotton gin, the profitable cultivation of cotton (over tobacco, rice, and indigo), using slave labor, spread the institution across Alabama and Mississippi. This made it more difficult for Jefferson to believe that slavery would simply "go away" by itself with the benign assistance of free markets and technological progress. And it made it increasingly difficult for Jefferson to separate his support for southern republicanism and its economic base of slavery agrarianism.[35] Hence, his famous

---

[33] Taylor, *Arator,* p. 115.

[34] Ibid. This view was "moderate" in antebellum Virginia when compared with the radical proslavery arguments of Taylor's Virginia neighbor George Fitzhugh, who, in *Cannibals All!* (1854), praised slavery as a moral institution beneficial to the slaves as well as the masters:

> The negro slaves of the South are the happiest, and, in some sense, the freest people in the world. The children and the aged and infirm work not at all, and yet have all the comforts and necessities of life provided for them. . . . The women do little hard work, and are protected from the despotism of their husbands by their masters. The negro man and stout boys work . . . not more than nine hours a day. The balance of their time is spent in perfect abandon . . . with their faces upturned to the sun, they can sleep at any hour (in Kenneth Dolbeare, *American Political Thought* [Monterey: Duxbury Press, 1981], pp. 287–88).

[35] Miller, *The Wolf by the Ears,* p. 125.

comment of the dilemma inherent in American slavery: "We have the wolf by the ears; and we can neither hold him, nor safely let him go. Justice is in one scale, and self-preservation in the other."[36]

Jefferson meant his own personal self-preservation as well as that of southern agrarian republicanism. In the new American republic, slaves constituted the largest property interest in the country, surpassed only by land itself, and vastly outweighing manufacturing or shipping. Virginia had gone from having just 6,000 black slaves in 1700 to having over 200,000 at the time of the Revolution; over half of the blacks in America were in Virginia.[37] By the time he wrote the Declaration of Independence, Jefferson was one of the wealthiest and largest slaveowners in Virginia. Yet by the end of his life, Jefferson, with most Virginia gentry, was near financial ruin: heavily in debt, drawing dwindling revenues from tobacco-exhausted soil and financially drained by a constant stream of houseguests enjoying the gracious hospitality of the squire of Monticello. As John Chester Miller wrote of the period: "Living opulently on their estates, surrounded by black servitors, and entertaining a constant stream of visitors, the members of the Virginia dynasty went down like gentlemen to financial ruin."[38] This led Jefferson, who repeatedly insisted that "there is nothing I would not sacrifice to a practicable plan of abolishing every vestige of this moral and political depravity," to increasingly hold on to his slaves for all they were worth.[39] It would seem that a "practicable" plan would involve not sacrificing the standard of living to which he had grown accustomed as a wealthy member of the Virginia gentry, nor threatening the republican virtue of southern whites. In Jefferson's hierarchy of values, the emancipation of slaves occupied a lower position than either his personal lifestyle or the ideal republic for which he had risked his life and fortune. Still, there echoed in Jefferson's late anxieties over the contradiction of hu-

---

[36]Ibid., frontispiece.
[37]Ibid., pp. 1–2.
[38]Ibid., p. 252.
[39]Ibid., p. 251.

man bondage in a republic of independent, active citizens his earlier unambiguous statement:

> Can the liberties of a nation be thought secure when we have removed their only firm basis, a conviction in the minds of the people that these liberties are the gift of God. That they are not to be violated but with his wrath? Indeed, I tremble for my country when I reflect that God is just; that his justice cannot sleep forever; that considering numbers, nature and natural means only, a revolution of the wheel of fortune, an exchange of situation is among possible events; that it may become probable by supernatural interference! The Almighty has no attribute which can take side with us in such a contest.[40]

In the end, Jefferson's ideas and actions on slavery, within the context of his political philosophy, may tell us more about the human capacity for self-deception than anything else.

---

[40] Jefferson, *Notes on the State of Virginia*, 8:404.

CHAPTER 9

THOMAS JEFFERSON
AS POLITICAL PHILOSOPHER:
FREEDOM, DEMOCRACY,
EQUALITY, RIGHTS

HAVING TRACED the development of Thomas Jefferson's political philosophy through the historical periods when America was a colony, a revolutionary state, and a new republic, employing the categories of human nature, political society, and social ethics found in classical republican and British liberal political theory, it is now possible to briefly define his conceptions of freedom, democracy, equality, and rights.

FREEDOM

Thomas Jefferson's understanding of freedom encompasses both the liberal, Lockean ideas of individual freedom from government interference and the classical notion of freedom to participate in the public deliberation which develops one's highest qualities and shapes the laws under which one lives. The seemingly contradictory position of adhering to both ancient and modern conceptions is reconciled by Jefferson's adaptation of Lockean freedom to serve the ends of classical freedom embodied in local democratic legislatures, and his belief that participatory republics would protect individual natural rights.

Jefferson's earliest and most familiar perception of freedom was expressed in the Declaration of Independence, and entails a freedom from arbitrary, tyrannical government defined according to Locke's psychology of free, equal, and independent individuals possessed of natural rights who must legitimately submit only to limited authority to which they consent in order to protect their material self-preservation. However, as we have seen, this liberal creed, designed by Locke for use by free and independent individuals in the state of nature, was adapted by Jefferson for free and independent states (first in the colonial legislatures and then in the state democracies) against the arbitrary and corrupt rule of distant, commercial regimes (first in the British Parliament and then in the federal government).

As such, Jefferson's use of the limited liberal conception of freedom was altered to signify not merely liberty from governmental tyranny over the individual, but liberty from centralized government's usurpation of local, democratic sovereignty. And Jefferson's invocation of Lockean freedom on behalf of small democratic republics followed from a nonliberal appreciation of the human psyche which understood that certain of the qualities of classical republics, like their cultivation of virtue through direct participation in community life, cannot be replicated in a large-scale, highly-centralized regime. That Jefferson had faith in a small-scale, participatory republic's ability to protect individual rights and liberties implies that he found the greatest threat to individual rights from remote, centralized government, not local or state government where citizens are more likely to be actively involved, rendering those governments more responsive and responsible. Jefferson's mature appreciation of freedom involved participation in the creation of the society of which the individual is a natural part. For if man is naturally a social being inevitably residing in a political society, true freedom does not consist merely in private liberty and detachment from the community, but in the realization of the individual's noblest qualities and submission to the laws he has helped to create.[1]

---

[1] Cf. Rousseau's definition of true liberty as "obedience to a law we prescribe

Hence, Jefferson's conception of freedom is not reducible solely to liberal procedural restraints premised in epistemological skepticism; rather it contains a substantive quality implying objective standards of goodness and justice. Jefferson argues for freedom of religion not because he believes that the essential ethical truths of Christianity are invalid or unknowable, but because he regards the free discussion of the various interpretations of Scripture as the most effective means of discovering and inculcating those essential religious truths. Similarly, Jefferson is not the staunchest advocate of the free press merely for the sake of abstract freedom, but because he believed that "freedom of the press . . . is the best instrument for enlightening the mind of man, and improving him as a rational, moral, and social being."[2] Thus, Jeffersonian freedom includes freedom from arbitrary rule and freedom to actively participate in shaping one's social destiny toward the end of more decent, intelligent, and contented citizens residing within a harmonious and just state. That is, Jefferson's notion of freedom leads directly into his conception of democracy.

DEMOCRACY

Jefferson's plan for small ward republics in which citizens regularly participate, along with that system of representation which grows out of local democracy and is characterized by a natural aristocracy of wisdom and virtue, was a classical conception of democracy, adapted to the vast American continent. It was founded on the assumption that man is naturally a social animal, capable of knowing and preserving the common good, and contrasts markedly with modern liberal democracy which relies on man's private interests and involves such strenuous citizenship as voting for representatives every two or four years. For Jef-

---

to ourselves," *The Social Contract,* ed. G. D. H. Cole (New York: Dutton, 1973), book 1, ch. 7, p. 174.

[2] Jefferson to Monsieur A. Coray, Oct. 31, 1823, in Jefferson, *The Writings of Thomas Jefferson,* 20 vols., ed. Albert Ellery Bergh (Washington, D.C.: Thomas Jefferson Memorial Assoc., 1904–05), 15:489.

ferson, this classical democracy of the ward republics provided the most efficient administration of public policy by cultivating the citizens' hearts and minds: by developing both their affectionate regard for the community and nation and their rational faculties requisite to wise public deliberation. Ward democracy accomplished this by cultivating man's "moral sense," which included both his innate sympathies and a capacity for moral reasoning, together producing man's knowledge of justice. To attain this advanced level of participation necessary for the development of the individual's moral sense and the citizens' appreciation of the natural aristocracy, Jefferson believed society must provide the educational, political, and economic means appropriate to such elevated democracy. Given these requisites, republican virtue might be safely extended to the increasingly centralized powers in county, state, and federal republics.

Of course, even with these requisites to virtuous democracy in the large nation, Jefferson's reliance upon a natural aristocracy of superior wisdom and virtue implies a basic inequality among citizens in those very traits which render them social. But this "mass elite" distinction in Jefferson's democratic theory is reconciled through the democratic selection of that aristocracy by an informed populace which does not regard that superiority as threatening when enlisted for the public good. And for Jefferson, the choice is not between living under an aristocracy and not living under an aristocracy; a vast representative democracy compels some form of ruling elite. The question is what sort of aristocracy is going to occupy that ruling position. A country consisting of small republics providing political freedom, educational opportunity, and economic equality will more likely produce representatives from the natural aristocracy of wisdom and virtue capable of knowing the common good; while a society lacking such requisites of classical democracy will more likely be governed by one of the artificial aristocracies of wealth or birth which, at best, is capable of knowing its own private good.

Thus, Jefferson's economically independent, educated, and active democratic citizenry was "virtuous" in both the functional and the moral sense of that Greek idea: it was qualified to function as a self-governing body (which is impossible under conditions of economic deprivation or dependence, ignorance or passivity) and it came, through such qualified self-governance, to see individual benefit in the common good. Again, Jefferson, perhaps naively, did not see any essential incompatibility between liberal natural rights and classical public virtue if society was properly ordered and individual citizens properly qualified.

EQUALITY

Jefferson may have asserted, in that oft-quoted phrase from the Declaration of Independence, that "all men are created equal"; but his mature writings suggest that he thought most men revealed their manifest inequality shortly after that creation. In the end, Jefferson regarded men as equal in some ways and unequal in others, but more important for his political theory, he believed that in a just society the inequalities among individuals were neither necessarily degrading nor injurious.

Jefferson considered men equal in the liberal sense of possessing common characteristics in the physical senses, material needs, and powers, and in the rights to self-preservation attending those corporal qualities. But he also considered men equal in the classical sense of being naturally social animals capable of moral choice and just action. Yet it was precisely in this classical definition of man's highest faculties that Jefferson emphasized the unequal distribution of the wisdom and virtue that makes social harmony and justice possible. The Jeffersonian equality which transcends both the liberal and classical distinctions among individuals resides in a common dependence on one another and a shared devotion to the public good. While the natural aristocracy is manifestly superior to the ordinary citizens in virtue and wisdom it depends on them for its own recognition and elevation into positions of public trust; and while the populace is admittedly limited in certain capacities, it is both worthy of its highest cultivation in democracy as a source of that aristocracy and a necessary check on its representatives through periodic election. While there remains a diversity of talents in the republic, a unity exists through shared contributions to the good of the whole of which each is a part; and while differences of quality persist among individuals, equality reigns through a common devotion to the public good.

RIGHTS

Jefferson's understanding of human rights is usually associated with Lockean natural rights protecting the individual from governmental incursion into one's self-preservation by securing life, liberty, and property. Yet Jefferson's most explicit articulation of the rights of man was in support of the American Bill of Rights, which he considered essential amendments to the United States Constitution. As noted earlier, Jefferson conceived of such rights as free speech and free press not as goods in themselves, but as necessary elements in the deliberative life of small republics. Without free speech, participatory democracy is a fiction; and without participatory democracy, man's social nature remains undeveloped. Thus, while Lockean rights tend to emphasize man's private interests and economic existence, Jeffersonian rights emphasize man's public nature and political life.

In addition to the formal rights necessary to public deliberation, Jefferson's mature political theory implies those substantive rights necessary to the realization of free speech, free press, free assembly, etc; that is, rights to an education suited to the individual's capacities, a measure of economic independence, and the opportunity to shape one's social destiny at the local community level. Put another way, Jefferson's theory implies the right to be free from inadequate education, degrading poverty, and bureaucratic fiat. If man's noblest quality is to be cultivated, and that quality resides in a moral sense enlightened by ethical teachings, another Jeffersonian right might be the opportunity to be exposed to, but not indoctrinated in, a variety of religious perspectives, as Jefferson recommended for the University of Virginia. Purely private economic rights, commonly justified on Lockean or Hamiltonian grounds, to accumulate unlimited amounts of material wealth and power unregulated by the society for the public good, seem not to be part of Jefferson's vision. That is, the Jeffersonian rights which are embodied in the first ten amendments to the American Constitution are addressed to the public activity of a naturally social being whose concerns extend beyond his own private interests.

THE POLITICAL THEORY of Thomas Jefferson is an original and distinctly American political theory. It is drawn, indeed, from the classics in ancient and modern political philosophy; but it is adapted to the unique conditions of the American experience. As with all political theory, broadly defined, Jefferson's political thought encompasses psychology, philosophy, economics, ethics, education, and religion within a single worldview. As a coherent vision devoted to freedom in the noblest sense, Jefferson's political theory provides a standard against which American political practice might be measured. Thomas Jefferson as a political philosopher was neither a pure materialist nor an absolute idealist; he was both. He applied the wisdom of the past to the crucial issues of the present in a creative, open-minded way. For this reason, his finest monument may in the end not be the Declaration of Independence, ward democracy, or economic progress, but the establishment of a university.

If we wish to continue flattering ourselves as "the nation of Jefferson," every generation of Americans is obliged to determine how well its society and values measure up to Jefferson's hope for the new American republic. Our current efforts to fully extend the rights, privileges, and obligations of citizenship to Americans neglected by Jefferson himself, notably blacks and women, are a part of the ongoing striving for the realization of that ideal republic.

APPENDIX

EARLY AMERICAN HISTORIOGRAPHY AND THE POLITICAL PHILOSOPHY OF THOMAS JEFFERSON

THE BEGINNING of the "republican revolution" in American historiography is usually dated at 1967, with the appearance of *The Ideological Origins of the American Revolution* by Harvard historian Bernard Bailyn.[1] This is despite the fact that, as Joyce Appleby points out, the word "republican" scarcely appears in the book.[2] It is also despite the fact that Bailyn finds Locke to be a pervasive influence in early American pamphlets and liberal natural rights philosophy an important factor in the American Revolution.[3] However, Bailyn detects another philosophical strain in colonial pamphlets and sermons—a sturdy republican virtue, enjoining simplicity and frugality.[4] He verifies traces of the English Country ideology in America expressing fear to the

---

[1] Bernard Bailyn, *The Ideological Origins of the American Revolution* (Cambridge, Mass.: Harvard University Press, 1967). See John Diggins, *The Lost Soul of American Politics* (New York: Basic Books, 1984), p. 366.

[2] Joyce Appleby, "Republicanism and Ideology," *American Quarterly* 37 (Fall 1985): 461–73, at 464.

[3] Bailyn, *The Ideological Origins of the American Revolution*, p. 27.

[4] Ibid., p. 25. John Diggins, in *The Lost Soul of American Politics*, finds such New England "virtue" attributable more to Puritan Calvinism and I am inclined to agree with him.

point of paranoia over British imperial wealth, luxury, extravagance, corruption, and tyranny—all indicating the reappearance of classical republican ideology.[5] Finally, Bailyn clears the way for a classical rendering of Thomas Jefferson by stating that while most American colonists used ancient authors "ornamentally," Jefferson was a "careful reader" of the Greek and Roman classics.[6]

Bailyn's prominent place in this new paradigm, however, is attributable more to the method of *The Ideological Origins of the American Revolution* than to its substance. For in it, Bailyn emphasizes the autonomous influence of ideas on revolutionary actions, in contrast with the progressive or Marxist historians who emphasized the social, economic, and institutional causes of political action, seeing ideas as merely reflections of these "concrete" material conditions. As Bailyn wrote in the preface to his award-winning book, "the American Revolution was above all else an ideological, constitutional, political struggle and not primarily a controversy between social groups undertaken to force changes in the organization of the society or the economy."[7] Or, as he explained in another work:

> the outbreak of the Revolution was not the result of social discontent, or of economic disturbances, or of rising misery, or of those mysterious social strains that seem to beguile the imaginations of historians straining to find peculiar predispositions to upheaval. [Rather,] American resistance in the 1760's and 1770's was a response to the acts of power deemed arbitrary, degrading, and uncontrollable—a response, in itself objectively reasonable, that was inflamed to the point of explosion by ideological currents generating fears everywhere in America that irresponsible and self-seeking adventurers—what the twentieth century would call political gangsters—had gained the power of the English government and were turning first, for reasons that were variously explained, to that Rhineland of their aggressions, the colonies.[8]

---

[5] Bailyn, *The Ideological Origins of the American Revolution*, pp. 48–50.
[6] Ibid., pp. 24–25.
[7] Ibid., p. vi.
[8] Bernard Bailyn, "The Central Themes of the American Revolution: An Interpretation," in *Essays on the American Revolution*, Stephen Kurtz and James Hutson, eds. (Chapel Hill: University of North Carolina Press, 1973), pp. 12–13.

Bailyn's emphasis on the autonomous influence of ideas and theories on political actions opened the door for more thorough study of the many philosophical influences on early American thought, including the ancient concepts underlying classical republicanism.

The really giant figure in this new paradigm is historian J. G. A. Pocock. He develops, in the course of almost thirty years of scholarship, the clearest definition of classical republicanism. For Pocock, this ideological tradition draws from Aristotle the conception of a naturally social man requiring economic independence to participate in political life and thereby develop his *telos* and the virtuous polis. From Machiavelli, this tradition continues a concern for ancient virtue and adds an appreciation of the Roman cycles of decay, death, and regeneration of the republic, along with a contempt for mercenary standing armies. From the English commonwealthsman James Harrington, this ideology adds an identification of ancient virtue and participation with a Country gentry civilization threatened by a corrupt court faction dominated by financial intrigue, political tyranny, and personal vice.[9] All of these philosophical progenitors of republicanism, for Pocock, share an affinity for the classical "mixed constitution" of the one (monarchy), the few (aristocracy), and the many (democracy), also associated with Montesquieu, as the most stable and just regime and the most important to defend by returning to original principles when threatened by corrupted politicians who seek to disturb the balance by concentrating all power and wealth in their central government.[10] As Pocock summarizes it in "Cambridge Paradigms and Scotch Philosophers":

[The] civic humanist paradigm . . . makes its starting point a certain early modern articulation of the idea of virtue. In this sense, the term "virtue" referred not simply to morally desirable practices or the inner disposition of the self towards them, but to the practice

---

[9] J. G. A. Pocock, *The Machiavellian Moment* (Princeton, N.J.: Princeton University Press, 1969); Pocock, "Machiavelli, Harrington and English Political Ideologies in the Eighteenth Century," *William and Mary Quarterly* 22 (October 1965): 549–83.

[10] Pocock, *The Machiavellian Moment*, p. 486; Z. S. Fink, *The Classical Republicans* (Evanston, Ill.: Northwestern University Press, 1945).

of citizenship in the classical or Graeco–Roman sense of that term. It entailed the maintenance of a civic equality among those who passed the often severe tests prerequisite to equality, and the moral disposition of the self towards the maintenance of a public (a better adjective than common) good, identifiable with the political association, *polis* or *respublica*, itself. It affirmed that the human personality was that of a *zōon politikon* and was fully expressed only in the practice of citizenship as an active virtue; man (the male bias of this ideal bordered on the absolute) was by nature a public being, and his public action was less that of a magistrate exercising authority than that of a citizen exercising equality. Authority occurred either as that of a master over an inferior, an equal over a non-equal—the classical republic was an open conspiracy of equals—or in a more moral sense, within the republic itself, as that of a few to which the many deferred without sacrificing their equality. And as the result of historical processes which need not be rehearsed again here, virtue in this sense had acquired material as well as moral preconditions. To qualify for equality and citizenship, the individual must be master of his own household, proprietor along with his equals of the only arms permitted to be borne in wars which must be publicly undertaken, and possessor of property whose function was to bring him not profit and luxury, but independence and leisure.[11]

For Pocock, this "Machiavellian moment" is of considerable duration. It reappears in the American Revolution, as the virtuous colonists resist the corrupt parliamentary empire and again when the virtuous Jeffersonians defeat the corrupt Hamiltonian Federalists. Accompanying this long moment is Pocock's insistence that the influence of Locke and natural rights liberalism is a "myth" in America, easily and correctly replaced by classical republican ideology.

It is notorious that American culture is haunted by myths, many of which arise out of the attempt to escape history and then regenerate it. The conventional wisdom among scholars who have studied their growth has been that the Puritan covenant was reborn in the Lockean contract, so that Locke himself has been elevated

---

[11] J. G. A. Pocock, "Cambridge Paradigms and Scotch Philosophers," in *Wealth and Virtue*, eds. Istvan Hont and Michael Ignatieff (Cambridge: Cambridge University Press, 1983), pp. 235–36.

to the station of a patron saint of American values and the quarrel
with history has been seen in terms of a constant attempt to escape
into the wilderness and repeat a Lockean experiment in the foundation of a natural society. The interpretation put forward here
stresses Machiavelli at the expense of Locke; it suggests that the
republic—a concept derived from Renaissance humanism—was the
true heir of the covenant and the dread of corruption the true heir
of the jeremiad. It suggests that the foundation of independent
America was seen, and stated, as taking place at a Machiavellian—
even a Rousseauean—moment, at which the fragility of the experiment, and the ambiguity of the republic's position in secular
time, was more vividly appreciated than it could have been from
a Lockean perspective.[12]

While the effect of Pocock's republican revision on Lockean
historiography has been considerable, it has not been accepted
as whole cloth, even by those who subscribe to its basic tenets.
A major study which accepted but modified the classical republican paradigm was Gordon Wood's *The Creation of the American
Republic*. In it, Wood examines the "pattern of ideas" in America
in the period between the American Revolution and the ratifi-
cation of the U.S. Constitution.[13] He finds that while republican
themes of political participation and public virtue such as fortitude, simplicity, and individual sacrifice for the common good
dominated the revolutionary and immediate postrevolutionary
periods, these gave way to more individualist, contractual, and
Lockean concepts as the Constitution was developed in response
to a "licentious" people incapable of living up to those standards
of virtue.[14] As a less than disciplined people were freed from the
authority of the Crown, there appeared in many areas (notably
Massachusetts) a kind of mobocracy, led by demagoguery and
espousing a radical egalitarian populism whose chief virtue was
an attack on any and all forms of superiority: of status, wealth,

---

[12]Pocock, *The Machiavellian Moment*, p. 545.
[13]Gordon Wood, *The Creation of the American Republic* (Chapel Hill: University
of North Carolina Press, 1969), p. viii.
[14]Ibid., pp. 475–508. Again, I am inclined to agree with Diggins that these
virtues sound more Puritan and Calvinist than classical republican. See also
Forrest McDonald, *Norvus Ordo Seclorum: The Intellectual Origins of the Constitution* (Lawrence: University Press of Kansas, 1985), p. viii.

education, or morality—effectively asserting a superiority of the lowest and meanest elements of society.[15] The authors of the *Federalist Papers* and supporters of the Constitution responded by instituting a government based on Lockean rights and protections of individual property and excellence, and not dependent upon the virtue of the common man.[16] Thus, for Wood, the American experiment began as classical republicanism, but ended as Lockean liberalism: "Although this Lockean notion of a social contract was not generally drawn upon by Americans in their dispute with Great Britain, for it had little relevance in explaining either the nature of their colonial charters or their relationship to the empire, it became increasingly meaningful in the years after 1776."[17]

Although Wood's *Creation of the American Republic* is a largely correct assessment of the general ideological trends in early America, my work takes issue with its application to the political philosophy of Thomas Jefferson, arguing almost the opposite of its thesis, by finding Jefferson Lockean in the revolutionary period and classical in the republican period. Contributing to my thesis is Lance Banning's *The Jeffersonian Persuasion,* which, while it accepts much of Wood's thesis that the Constitution is liberal, qualifies it with the claim that republicanism lived on in "opposition" Jeffersonians, who ultimately triumphed in the presidential administrations of Jefferson, Madison, and Monroe.[18] Several other scholars have concurred with Banning's agreement with Wood's general assessment of the Constitution's liberalism, but with the continuation of classical republicanism as an alternative undercurrent in American political thought and practice.[19]

---

[15] Wood, *The Creation of the American Republic,* pp. 400–25.

[16] Ibid., pp. 467–85. See also Albert Furtwangler, *The Authority of Publius* (Ithaca: Cornell University Press, 1984).

[17] Wood, *The Creation of the American Republic,* p. 283. This is not the case with Jefferson's Declaration of Independence; see ch. 4.

[18] Lance Banning, *The Jeffersonian Persuasion* (Ithaca: Cornell University Press, 1978), p. 93. See also Banning, "Jeffersonian Ideology Revisited: Liberal and Classical Ideas in the New American Republic," *William and Mary Quarterly* 43 (January 1986): 3–19.

[19] Isaac Kramnick, "Republican Revisionism Revisited," *American Historical Review* 87 (June 1982): 629–64, at 664.

Princeton historian John Murrin relates this thesis to the earlier English experience and argues for a "great inversion" in America.[20] While in the English Whig revolution of 1688–1721, the Court ideology of public credit and financial corruption triumphed, Murrin finds the American Revolution of 1776–1816 to be a victory of Jeffersonian Country virtue over Hamiltonian Court intrigue. He attributes this prevalance of republicanism to the influence of the Virginia gentry (with strong traditions of economic independence and participatory citizenship) in the founding and early republican periods.[21]

Drew McCoy's *The Elusive Republic: Political Economy in Jeffersonian America,* accepts this classical republican interpretation of early American ideology, but wrestles, successfully I think, with the problem of reconciling a nostalgic agrarian economic stance, requisite to an independent, virtuous citizenry, with the growth of commerce and a free market economy in nineteenth-century America. McCoy reconciles these disparate strands of early American ideology by showing that Jefferson accepted certain kinds of economic development which he thought complemented republican virtue.[22] Specifically, Jefferson found advances in agricultural production, home manufacture, and free trade noninjurious to the economic independence and political virtue of the American citizenry. Such advances further enhanced the American republic by rendering it self-sufficient economically and therefore independent of corrupting British finance and imperialism. The type of economic development that Jeffersonians found unacceptable was the banking, stockjobbing, and urban manufacture that corroded the economic independence of the citizen and the country and handed over both to British cor-

---

[20] John M. Murrin, "The Great Inversion, or Court versus Country," in *Three British Revolutions, 1641, 1688, 1776,* ed. J. G. A. Pocock (Princeton, N.J.: Princeton University Press, 1980).

[21] Murrin, "The Great Inversion, or Court versus Country," p. 426.

[22] Drew McCoy, *The Elusive Republic: Political Economy in Jeffersonian America* (Chapel Hill: University of North Carolina Press, 1980), pp. 10, 67, 186, 144. This problem is raised most forcefully in Joyce Appleby, "Republicanism in Old and New Contexts," *William and Mary Quarterly* 43 (January 1986): 20–34, see pp. 31–34.

ruption.[23] This analysis furthered my own assessment of the role of modern economics in Jefferson's political philosophy.

Although Garry Wills's book, *Inventing America,* is not part of the classical republican literature and has been described by Harvard's Judith Shklar as "terrible intellectual history,"[24] it should probably be mentioned here as part of the anti-Lockean revision to early American historiography. Wills argues that Jefferson's Declaration of Independence was not Lockean in character, but rather grounded in the Scottish moral sense philosophy of Lord Kames, Thomas Reid, and Thomas Hutchinson. Jefferson ostensibly imbibed this philosophy from the Scotsman, Professor Small, at the College of William and Mary. The Scottish moral sense philosophers challenged Lockean individualism by situating a sense of sympathy and benevolence in human beings, which rendered them naturally social. By making ethics a matter of a physical sense, these philosophers were able to beat the liberal materialists at their own game, without having to refer to discredited medieval Thomist ethics and authority.[25] Despite its popular readership, Wills's thesis that Jefferson employed this philosophy in the Declaration of Independence was found entirely unpersuasive in the scholarly community. The brilliant flaw in his argument is that the moral sense philosophy appeared not in Jefferson's revolutionary writings, but in his postrevolutionary political philosophy, as Matthews and McDonald have shown, and as I have developed in this book.[26]

CRITIQUES OF CLASSICAL REPUBLICANISM

Although the classical republican paradigm has had an enormous impact upon the way we perceive early American political

---

[23] McCoy, *The Elusive Republic,* pp. 152, 249.

[24] Judith Shklar in *New Republic,* 26 August and 2 Sept. 1978, p. 32.

[25] Garry Wills, *Inventing America: Jefferson's Declaration of Independence* (New York: Doubleday, 1978), pp. 193–96.

[26] Richard Matthews, *The Radical Politics of Thomas Jefferson* (Lawrence: University Press of Kansas, 1984), pp. 58–59; McDonald, *Novus Ordo Seclorum,* p. viii.

thought, and especially the political theory of Thomas Jefferson, it has not been without its critics. Several scholars have contested its theses by reasserting the influence of Locke on early American ideology, by showing internal inconsistencies within the paradigm, or by questioning its applicability to specific thinkers, policies, or institutions.[27]

The historian Joyce Appleby is probably the foremost critic of the classical republican paradigm, although she acknowledges its force as an alternative ideology in a predominantly Lockean constitutional system and modern, capitalist market economy in America. Appleby also argues that Jefferson is not within the republican tradition. In general, Appleby insists that early American society was congenial with political liberalism and its economic corollary, free market capitalism, because both liberated the common man from traditional authority and the hierarchy of class and place.[28] The freedom of opportunity offered by early capitalism, with its free movement of persons and ideas, its latitude for economic achievement and upward mobility, and its rewards for hard work and creativity regardless of social background, seemed glorious when compared with the rigid social hierarchy and stodgy attitude toward change in traditional eighteenth-century society. When such economic freedom was combined with a liberal, limited state which guaranteed natural rights to life, liberty, and property and allowed freedom of speech, press, assembly, and belief, it seemed even more attractive, especially compared with the harsh and arbitrary traditional regime. Such liberalism and capitalism in early America engaged common Americans more than any nostalgic, communitarian republicanism, with its emphasis on political participation and public virtue.[29]

Appleby further argues that Jefferson is especially unsuited to

---

[27] See Robert E. Shalhope, "Republicanism and Early American Historiography," *William and Mary Quarterly* 39 (April 1982): 334–56. For a new and extensive critique of this paradigm, see Steven Dworetz, *The Unvarnished Doctrine: Locke, Liberalism and the American Revolution* (Durham, N.C.: Duke University Press, 1990).

[28] Joyce Appleby, *Capitalism and a New Social Order* (New York: New York University Press, 1984), pp. 50–53.

[29] Ibid., pp. 86, 97.

the characterization as a classical republican, because he did not look to the past for wisdom, but to the future for new possibilities; he did not want neatly ordered social relations—which he associated with medieval tyranny and entrenched aristocracy; he did not celebrate political participation, but loved domestic tranquility; and he was favorably inclined toward Lockean natural rights philosophy and free market capitalism.[30] Finally, Appleby finds Jefferson heavily influenced by the French political economist Destutt de Tracy, whose liberal vision of human nature, faith in progress and economic development, and celebration of private life is not compatible with classical republican thought.[31] Despite this thorough critique of classical republicanism and its application to Thomas Jefferson, however, Appleby admits that something called "republicanism" did exist in early American thought, and served as a more communitarian alternative to liberal and capitalist individualism and freedom.[32]

Richard Matthews's *The Radical Politics of Thomas Jefferson* critiques the classical republican paradigm without returning to Lockean orthodoxy. His treatment of Jefferson's political theory is one of the most interesting and provocative available. It agrees with the civic humanist view that Jefferson was Aristotelean in his notion of social man and participatory democracy, but rejects the backward-looking nostalgia of that paradigm. He agrees with Appleby that Jefferson was not opposed to modernity, but challenges her interpretation that he favored capitalism.[33]

Matthews finds Jefferson using concepts from Scottish moral sense philosophy, Aristotelean and Rousseauian political theory, and radical democracy to produce a society of educated, economically independent, self-determining communities that engage in perpetual revolution as ideas and institutions fail to keep up with the progress of knowledge and technology. For Matthews, an enlightened, sensitive, and economically self-deter-

---

[30] Joyce Appleby, "Republicanism in Old and New Contexts," *William and Mary Quarterly* 43 (January 1986): 20–34, at 25, 34.

[31] Joyce Appleby, "What Is Still American in the Political Philosophy of Thomas Jefferson?" *William and Mary Quarterly* 39 (April 1982): 287–309.

[32] Appleby, "Republicanism and Ideology," 472.

[33] Matthews, *The Radical Politics of Thomas Jefferson*, pp. 5–7, 12–15.

mining citizenry would place primacy on community interest over private economic gain and human cooperation over an avaricious market capitalism.[34]

> Recognizing the need for every generation to begin anew, Jefferson's open-ended political philosophy actively encourages individuals, within the guidelines of political participation, economic freedom, and moral responsibility, to create and re-create community. These celebrations of democratic community, moreover, simultaneously provide a good opportunity to redistribute property, thereby protecting an individual's economic independence. They also keep the society in a state of constant revolution, in harmony with human and social evolution. Participatory democracy in both the political realm and the economic realm is, to Jefferson, a necessary prerequisite to human fulfillment.[35]

Forrest McDonald's *Novus Ordo Seclorum: The Intellectual Origins of the Constitution,* critiques the classical republican paradigm (especially J. G. A. Pocock) by asserting that several different kinds of "republican" ideology existed in early America, depending on the social and economic norms of various regions (notably New England Puritan and southern agrarian); that republicanism neglects the important influence of Scottish moral sense philosophy in several early American thinkers; and that classical republicanism depreciates Locke so much that it virtually eliminates the significant presence of natural rights philosophy in the American Revolution and founding.

A seminal critique of the republican revision was Isaac Kramnick's article, "Republican Revisionism Revisited," in the *American Historical Review* of 1982.[36] Kramnick, a prominent historian of eighteenth-century English political thought,[37] argues that while the classical republican paradigm illuminates an important alternative ideological strain, "in seeking to free the entire eighteenth century of Locke, of socioeconomic radicalism, and of bourgeois liberalism, this new broom has also swept away much

---

[34] Ibid., pp. 119–23.
[35] Ibid., p. 126.
[36] Kramnick, "Republican Revisionism Revisited."
[37] See Isaac Kramnick, *Bolingbroke and His Circle* (Cambridge, Mass.: Harvard University Press, 1968).

that is true."[38] Kramnick reveals the prevalence of Lockean liberalism in Britain and America, evidenced by, among other things, the enormous Tory reaction to it. When several Anglican Bishops are at pains to refute the radical ideas in Locke's *Second Treatise,* it is probably safe to assume that those ideas were having some impact.[39] Kramnick's theoretical clarification of various concepts used by the republican school—distinguishing between the Tory Aristotle and the Classical Aristotle and the various uses of the English Ancient Constitution—provides a very effective critique of several aspects of the republican paradigm.[40] Kramnick concludes, after the fashion of Mark Twain, that the "death" of Locke at the hands of the classical republicans is "greatly exaggerated."[41]

More recently, John Diggins's brilliant book, *The Lost Soul of American Politics,* critiqued the classical republican school by finding Lockean liberalism in two distinct places in the American tradition: (1) in Jefferson's revolutionary writings, particularly the Declaration of Independence, and (2) in the Federalists' (Madison and Hamilton's) influence on the U.S. Constitution.[42] Diggins provides possibly the most devastating critique of the republican interpretation of the Revolution by writing a mock Declaration of Independence using classical republican concepts and language.[43] Additionally, he argues that Calvinist Christianity explains much in American political culture and ideology, complementing Lockean notions of government while tempering the liberal's individualism and acquisitiveness.[44] Finally, Thomas Pangle's *The Spirit of Modern Republicanism* (1988) and Steven Dworetz's *The Unvarnished Doctrine: Locke, Liberalism and the American Revolution* (1990) reassert the influence of Locke on early American thinkers through close textual analysis of colonists' writings.[45]

---

[38] Kramnick, "Repubican Revisionism Revisited," p. 633.
[39] Ibid., p. 651.
[40] Ibid., pp. 634, 653.
[41] Ibid., p. 655.
[42] Diggins, *The Lost Soul of American Politics,* p. 5.
[43] Ibid., pp. 364–65.
[44] Ibid., pp. 7–9.
[45] Thomas Pangle, *The Spirit of Modern Republicanism* (Chicago: University of

PROBLEMATICAL ISSUES IN CLASSIFYING
JEFFERSON'S POLITICAL PHILOSOPHY

Despite the insights of Lockean orthodoxy, classical republicanism, and the critiques of classical republicanism in understanding early American political thought, and their contributions to my treatment of Thomas Jefferson's political philosophy, I have found several problems with their approaches from the perspective of political philosophy.

Problems with Lockean Orthodoxy

The Lockean orthodoxy which dominated early American studies for so many years viewed the American Revolution and founding through the concepts of natural rights held by free and equal individuals establishing a limited government to protect those rights through a social contract and reserving the right to revolution whenever the government failed to do its duty, or worse, invaded the rights of the citizens itself. This was the ideology that easily explained our American origins. As Joyce Appleby wrote: "Like a fish unaware of water we American writers have moved about in a world of invisible liberal assumptions."[46]

The first and most obvious deficiency of this view, as recent scholarship has demonstrated, is its failure to acknowledge other, non-Lockean, sources of early American ideology. These alternative ideologies might be considered contrary to the Lockean orthodoxy for a number of reasons: they may conceive of human nature in social or ethical or spiritual terms contrary to Locke's solitary, free, material, and self-interested model; they may conceive of society as coming together in ways other than through a rational social contract; or, they may conceive of the state as something more than a limited, liberal protector of individual rights. Ideologies that offer all these alternatives to Lockean liberalism were present in early American culture and philosophy.

The first non-Lockean ideology that we might consider is the

Chicago Press, 1988); Steven Dworetz, *The Unvarnished Doctrine* (Durham, N.C.: Duke University Press, 1990).

[46]Appleby, "Republicanism and Ideology," p. 471.

older Tory or Country thought which challenged liberalism with certain Aristotelean notions of man and society. Isaac Kramnick's *Bolingbroke and His Circle* describes this Tory ideology and its prevalence in eighteenth-century England. Drawing on a more Thomist worldview, this ideology of the landed gentry emphasized man's social nature and his natural place within a universal hierarchy. It regarded the individualism and capitalism implicit in Locke's philosophy as corrupt and venal, especially in the financial practices of the Walpole government.[47] Though we now take much of Lockean liberalism for granted, Locke's own age regarded it as new and radically dangerous.[48] The Tory ideology, with its emphasis upon landed property, social hierarchy, hereditary privilege and order, was also prevalent in Jefferson's Virginia, forming a culture not altogether congenial with Locke's *Second Treatise.*[49]

A second nonliberal strain in early American thought is Protestant Christianity, especially Calvinism. John Diggins, Gordon Wood, and Forrest McDonald all focus on the influence of this theology, which, although Max Weber's *The Protestant Ethic and the Spirit of Capitalism* has been seen as a religious corollary of liberal modernity, nevertheless tempered the stark individualism, materialism, and acquisitiveness of Locke's thought.[50] Wilson Carey McWilliams's monumental *The Idea of Fraternity in America* traces the movement of this influence throughout American politics, culture, and literature. While Thomas Jefferson rejected his own Anglican upbringing and sharply criticized Catholics and Calvinists, he possessed a deep personal faith in Christianity and placed an importance on Christian ethics to the American

---

[47]Kramnick, *Bolingbroke and His Circle.*

[48]C. B. Macpherson, *Democratic Theory* (Oxford: Clarendon Press, 1973), p. 225.

[49]McDonald, *Novus Ordo Seclorum,* pp. 11, 71; Murrin, "The Great Inversion," p. 426. Rhys Isaac, *The Transformation of Virginia, 1740–1790* (Chapel Hill: Univerity of North Carolina Press, 1982), pp. 44–64.

[50]Wood, *The Creation of the American Republic,* p. 7; Diggins, *The Lost Soul of American Politics,* pp. 7–9; McDonald, *Novus Ordo Seclorum,* pp. viii, 70; Max Weber, *The Protestant Ethic and the Spirit of Capitalism* (New York: Charles Scribner's Sons, 1958); Wilson Carey McWilliams, *The Idea of Fraternity in America* (Berkeley: University of California Press, 1973).

republic far outweighing his more orthodox brethren (such as John Adams).[51]

Another ideological strain challenging the Lockean view was Scottish moral sense philosophy. Elucidated in recent scholarship by McDonald, Matthews, and Wills, this eighteenth-century philosophy challenged the Lockean conception of human nature by positing a naturally social being stimulated to care for others by a sense of sympathy and benevolence.[52] By situating this social and ethical capacity in a sense, like sight, hearing, or touch, these philosophers appealed to Enlightenment materialists as well as more traditional thinkers.[53]

The presence of a classical republican ideology, premised in Aristotelean psychology and politics, has challenged the Lockean orthodoxy perhaps more than any other alternative thought in early America. This Aristotle is not that of medieval Thomism or the Tory Bolingbroke, with their emphasis on social hierarchy and authority.[54] Rather, the classical republican thought of Harrington and Jefferson draws upon those parts of Aristotle's *Politics* that define citizenship as direct participation in political life, requiring an economically independent citizenry, developing naturally social faculties in reasoned speech and moral choice, and creating standards of public virtue and excellence.[55]

A final problem for Lockean orthodoxy has to do with the manner in which scholars of this school apply Lockean natural rights philosophy to the American Revolution and founding, namely literally. Scholars such as Louis Hartz and Carl Becker, who accept the influence of Locke on American thinkers, tend to accept that transference as pure and unmodified.[56] My ar-

---

[51] Diggins notes this irony in *The Lost Soul of American Politics,* p. 79.

[52] McDonald, *Novus Ordo Seclorum,* pp. viii, 53–54; Matthews, *The Radical Politics of Thomas Jefferson,* pp. 45, 53, 58–59; Wills, *Inventing America,* pp. 175, 189.

[53] Kramnick, *Bolingbroke and His Circle,* pp. 86–87.

[54] Ibid., pp. 80–83. See also Garrett Ward Sheldon, *The History of Political Theory: Ancient Greece to Modern America* (New York: Peter Lang, 1988), ch. 6.

[55] Pocock, *The Machiavellian Moment,* pp. 67–68.

[56] Louis Hartz, *The Liberal Tradition in America* (New York: Harcourt Brace, 1955); Carl Becker, *The Declaration of Independence: A Study in the History of Political Ideas* (New York: Random House, 1958).

gument is that Jefferson did not always adopt purely the psychology and political theory of the *Second Treatise,* but adapted it to the contingencies of revolutionary colonies, and that this is clearest in the Declaration of Independence. Thus, while we find the presence of Locke in the Declaration unmistakable, it may not be quite the same Locke as that meant by Becker when he proclaimed that "Jefferson copied Locke."

Problems with Classical Republicanism

From the perspective of political philosophy there are several problems with the classical republican paradigm. These include a too vague definition of classical "virtue"; a too casual mixing of Machiavelli with Greek classicism; the inclusion of some liberal concepts and thinkers in this classical paradigm; and the use of the Ancient Constitution in contradictory ways.

The classical republican paradigm claims that virtue meant an unselfish concern for the public good.[57] But classical Greek and Roman political philosophy understood public virtue in a number of ways. Plato's conception of virtue, or *arete,* was a functional standard—a thing was virtuous because it possessed qualities enabling it to function well or effectively. A virtuous knife has the quality of sharpness because its function is to cut. A virtuous horse is swift because its function is to run.[58] Plato applied this functional standard of virtue to society through his division of the Republic into classes possessing specific virtues: rulers possess the virtues of wisdom and goodness; soldiers should have courage, honor, strength, frugality, and loyalty; and workers should be temperate and moderate.[59] Public virtue for Plato is made up of the virtues of different functionaries in society. The ruler, or philosopher-king, must have the virtue of wisdom, which is the knowledge of all the virtues in society and their proper ordering.

---

[57] Pocock, "Cambridge Paradigms and Scotch Philosophers," pp. 235–36; Pocock, *The Machiavellian Moment,* p. 201; Wood, *The Creation of the American Republic,* pp. 50–53.

[58] Plato, *The Apology,* trans. Hugh Tredennick (New York: Penguin, 1981); Plato, *The Republic,* trans. Allan Bloom (New York: Basic Books, 1968), p. 12. See Sheldon, *The History of Political Theory,* ch. 2.

[59] Plato, *The Republic,* p. 105.

Through a system of public education, the individual's unique virtues are identified, cultivated, and ordered harmoniously with the virtues of others. Justice is this ordering or giving each his "due" by developing and utilizing each citizen's skills for the good of the whole society.

Aristotle accepts the Platonic functional definition of virtue, but adds another conception: moral virtue or *ethike*.[60] Moral virtue governs purely human relations apart from individuals' social functions and requires a different kind of excellence. The Aristotelean virtuous or excellent man in this sense is one who knows and habitually practices the golden mean: is generous, as opposed to stingy or extravagant, witty, as opposed to boorish or buffoon-like.[61] The knowledge of moral virtue requires friendship and citizenship, or participation in public life.[62] This, in turn, requires a citizenry with economic independence, so that their political participation can concern the common good as opposed to private economic interest.[63]

The Roman conception of virtue, as expressed in Cicero, is different still. Cicero, concerned with the decadence, luxury, and drift toward tyranny of the expanding Roman Empire, strove to return Rome to its early republican virtues of sacrifice, honor, fortitude, and frugality.[64] But these Roman virtues are essentially military in nature—what Plato would have regarded as virtues of the soldier class—imposed on the whole society. This may be logical for the Roman Empire, but it does not reflect the highest Greek virtues.

Machiavelli's revival of "civic virtue" during the Renaissance is of this Roman, Ciceronian quality.[65] In his *Discourses*, Machiavelli elevates the traditional Roman virtues of sacrifice, honor,

---

[60] Aristotle, *Nicomachean Ethics*, trans. Martin Ostwald (Indianapolis: Bobbs-Merrill, 1962), p. 33; Sheldon, *The History of Political Theory*, pp. 44–45.

[61] Aristotle, *Nicomachean Ethics*, pp. 44–49.

[62] Aristotle, *The Politics*, trans. T. A. Sinclair (Baltimore: Penguin, 1972), pp. 28–29, 114.

[63] Ibid., p. 4.

[64] Cicero, *The Republic* and *The Laws*, trans. Clinton Keyes (Cambridge: Harvard University Press, 1928); Sheldon, *The History of Political Theory*, ch. 4.

[65] Quentin Skinner, *The Foundations of Modern Political Thought* (Cambridge: Cambridge University Press, 1978), pp. 88–94.

strength, and frugality for reasons very similar to Cicero's—to unite divided Italian provinces and city-states, thereby restoring a powerful Roman Empire.[66] Plato's highest virtues of "wisdom and goodness" in rulers and Aristotle's moral virtue of the excellent man, requiring friendship, citizenship and participation in the common good, do not exist in Machiavelli's conception of "virtue." Hence, J. G. A. Pocock's classical republican paradigm of "Aristotelean-Machiavellian"[67] civic humanism is seriously flawed. This casual mixing of Machiavelli, considered the first great modern theorist for his pessimism over human nature and his reliance on ruthless, deceitful power politics, with the optimism and ethical ideals of Plato and Aristotle, calls into question the value of much of Pocock's paradigm. Although Pocock undoubtedly uses James Harrington's description of Machiavelli as a "disciple" of the ancients to justify his inclusion in "civic humanism,"[68] Kramnick shows that the eighteenth-century attitude toward Machiavelli was highly ambivalent.[69] In contrast to Plato's vision of wise and good rulers or Aristotle's polis of excellent men, Machiavelli (in the *Discourses*) gives us this view of human nature and political leadership:

> It was a saying of ancient writers, that men afflict themselves in evil, and become weary of the good, and that both these dispositions produce the same effects. For when men are no longer obliged to fight from necessity, they fight from ambition, which passion is so powerful in the hearts of men that it never leaves them, no matter to what height they may rise. The reason of this is that nature has created men so that they desire everything, but are unable to attain it; desire being thus always greater than the faculty of acquiring, discontent with what they have and dissatisfaction with themselves result from it.[70]

---

[66] Machiavelli, *The Prince and the Discourses*, trans. Luigi Ricci, rev. by E. R. P. Vincent (New York: Random House, 1950), pp. 97–98.

[67] Pocock claims that Machiavelli's military virtue is the same as Aristotle's political virtue because both serve the good of the whole (*The Machiavellian Moment*, pp. 201–3).

[68] James Harrington, *Oceana*, ed. S. B. Liljegren (Westport, Conn.: Hyperion Press, 1979), p. 13.

[69] Kramnick, *Bolingbroke and His Circle*, pp. 163–65.

[70] Machiavelli, *The Prince and the Discourses*, p. 208.

With this lesson about human nature from the "ancient writers," Machiavelli goes on to advise the founders of states, again from *The Discourses* (not *The Prince*): "whoever desires to found a state and give it laws, must start with assuming that all men are bad and ever ready to display their vicious nature, whenever they may find occasion for it. If their evil disposition remains concealed for a time, it must be attributed to some unknown reason."[71] The danger of attempting to separate Machiavelli's *Prince*, which contains the deceitful power politics, from his *Discourses*, which supposedly is a fountain of public virtue and civic humanism, is obvious. The more traditional view in political theory (before the classical republican revolution) of marking the end of classicism with Cicero and associating Machiavelli, along with Hobbes, with the beginning of modernity, provides, in my view, much greater theoretical clarity.[72] Despite this problem, the classical republican connection of the ancients with James Harrington is much more valid and was exceptionally valuable in my analysis of Jefferson's political philosophy.

Another problem in the classical republican paradigm, which comes from a lack of theoretical clarity, is the combining in the republican tradition of several disparate thinkers in this ostensibly anti-Lockean school of thought—some of whom are more Lockean than classical. Carolyn Robbins's book, *The Eighteenth-Century Commonwealthsmen*, foreshadows this difficulty, as she explains that republicans are concerned with natural rights and corruption but fails to show how these republican natural rights differ from the Lockean natural rights that later classical republican historiographers claim republicans provide an alternative to.[73] Robbins enumerates the members of the Republican Club

---

[71] Ibid., p. 117.

[72] Pocock admits that his use of Machiavelli is selective and that "there will be aspects of Machiavelli's thought in *Il Principe* not dealt with here" (*Machiavellian Moment*, p. 157). I think, however, that his repeated references to "Aristotelean-Machiavellian" civic virtue are deceptive and that he should distinguish more clearly Machiavelli's precise place within this "classical" paradigm.

[73] Carolyn Robbins, *The Eighteenth-Century Commonwealthsmen* (Cambridge, Mass.: Harvard University Press, 1959), p. viii. Z. S. Fink, *Classical Republicans* (p. viii), avoids later theoretical dilemmas by defining the republican ideal simply in the terms of "a state which was not headed by a king and in which the

as including Aristotle, Cicero, Machiavelli, Harrington, and Sidney. This membership is largely accepted by later classical republican writers, including Bailyn and Pocock. But as with Machiavelli, political philosophy would find other figures unlikely members in this classical club. Algernon Sidney is perhaps the most glaring example of the fact that the classical republican paradigm makes for strange bedfellows. Sidney is traditionally considered one of the closest theorists to Locke in seventeenth-century England, a similarity which prompted Locke to leave the country shortly after Sidney was executed for publishing treasonous tracts. Although Sidney speaks of Roman virtue throughout his *Discourses Concerning Government,* it is always in terms of the natural rights, consensual government, and liberty associated with Lockean liberalism.[74] The likelihood, as Bailyn notes, is that many seventeenth and eighteenth-century English and American thinkers used classical, especially Roman, terms ornamentally to dress up their liberalism with antiquity, without regard for the theoretical inconsistencies entailed in such casual mixing of ancient and modern ideas.[75] The threat to our misunderstanding of American political principles is greatly exacerbated by this tendency to casually blend classical and liberal thinkers in the "non-Lockean" republican paradigm.

A related problem is the inclusion of the venerable English Ancient Constitution in the classical republican paradigm, as yet another non-Lockean element in our tradition.[76] As Pocock brilliantly shows in his first book, *The Ancient Constitution and the Feudal Law,* this fictitious conception of an ancient Saxon constitution in England was largely the invention of clever parliamentary lawyers, who used its antiquity to challenge the legit-

---

hereditary principle did not prevail." Both Fink and Robbins avoid many of the embarrassments of later classical republican scholars by not insisting that these eighteenth-century English thinkers employ classical ideas to the exclusion of liberal Lockean ideas.

[74] Algernon Sidney, *Discourses Concerning Government* (1698; New York: Arno Press, 1979), pp. 23, 112, 151, 242.

[75] Bailyn, *The Ideological Origins of the American Revolution,* pp. 24–25.

[76] Robbins, *The Eighteenth-Century Commonwealthsmen;* Appleby, "What is Still American," p. 289; Diggins, *The Lost Soul of American Politics,* pp. 31–33; Kramnick, "Republican Revisionism Revisited," p. 634.

imacy of a monarch whose authority rested on tradition and heredity.[77] This Ancient Constitution, therefore, was essentially a historical argument for liberal parliamentary claims to rights and liberty. It was from these parliamentary lawyers (including Coke and Blackstone) that Jefferson, studying for the bar in Virginia one hundred years later, learned of it and used it in his arguments against the Crown Empire. Pocock shows that when the Crown's historians demonstrated the fictitious qualities of the Ancient Constitution, parliamentarians began basing their rights and liberties on Nature (that is, Locke), which was not so easily refuted by the king. Jefferson goes through essentially the same process one hundred years later, when his early revolutionary justifications based on the Ancient Constitution began to get into historical hot water with respect to the royal colonial charters and he switched to the more amorphous natural rights philosophy found in Locke. All of this suggests the continuation of royal absolutist ideology in the American colonies and the corresponding revolutionary resistance on the basis of the English arguments of 1660–1688. The classical republican paradigm identifies the source of American revolutionary thought with the English period of 1688–1740, when the parliamentary Whigs were in command and, especially under Walpole, instituted all the financial reforms that Tories like Bolingbroke attacked as "corruption."[78] According to Pocock, therefore, the American revolutionary republican ideology is really Tory, against the corrupt modern practices of a Whig Parliament. I, on the other hand, find American revolutionary ideology, especially in Jefferson, drawing upon the anti-absolutist English ideology of 1660–1688 in the liberal Ancient Constitution and the liberal Lockean natural rights philosophy. The classical republican identification of the Ancient Constitution as anti-Lockean and its depreciation of its, and the colonies', anti-absolutist ideology in favor of the virtue of civic humanism distort the fundamental ideas prevalent at the time.

The final problem of classical republican thought is its denial

---

[77] J. G. A. Pocock, *The Ancient Constitution and the Feudal Law* (Cambridge: Cambridge University Press, 1951).

[78] See Kramnick, *Bolingbroke and His Circle*.

of any Lockean influence on the American Revolution and early republican periods. While this study finds classical qualities in his later political philosophy (sans Machiavelli), it is extreme to claim, as Pocock does, that classical republican ideology "altogether replaces" the presence of Locke in early America.[79] The often-cited founder of the classical republican paradigm, Bernard Bailyn in *The Ideological Origins of the American Revolution,* does not go that far, as he presents a balanced account of both Lockean and classical threads in early American ideology. The term "mythical," which Pocock uses to describe the American affinity for Lockean ideas, may, in the end, serve better to describe portions of his own classical republican paradigm.

Problems with the Critique of Classical Republicanism

The critics of classical republicanism tend to be more gracious than their republican opponents in accepting alternative influences on early American political thought, even while reasserting the presence of Locke. As Isaac Kramnick admits of eighteenth-century English and American thinkers, they "knew their Aristotle, their Machiavelli, and their Montesquieu," but "they also knew their Locke."[80] Appleby and Diggins have correctly reasserted the presence of Locke in Jefferson's Declaration of Independence, but have not examined how his political thought may have changed in the postrevolutionary period. The openness with which the critics of republicanism approach the multiple influences upon early American thought and culture, however, is congenial with my finding in Jefferson's mature political philosophy a coherent blending of liberalism, classicism, moral sense psychology, and Christian ethics.

Matthews illuminates many aspects of that core of Jefferson's thought and my analysis in many ways merely extends those aspects back in time to the colonial and revolutionary periods and forward to the anti-Federalist period. A final problem for Jefferson scholarship, noted by Matthews, is the frequent ten-

---

[79] Pocock, *The Machiavellian Moment,* p. 509.
[80] Kramnick, "Republican Revisionism Revisited," p. 664.

dency to equate Jefferson with "Jeffersonian."[81] Just as Karl Marx claimed that he was many things, but not a "Marxist," I think that we should be careful not to project back onto Jefferson the ideas and policies of his many associates and followers. While this book does not take on the ambitious task of separating all of Jefferson's theories from all the Jeffersonian ones, it may contribute to that future task by clarifying with greater precision those qualities in Jefferson's original political philosophy.

Finally, two recent books challenge the whole Lockean liberal-classical republican controversy by asserting a synthesis of the two theoretical strains, operating simultaneously, within early American ideology, affirming my conception of a mixture in Jefferson's political philosophy. Michael Lienesch's *New Order of the Ages* finds that "the truth lies somewhere in between. . . . in the late eighteenth century, American political thought was in transition, moving from classical republicanism to modern liberalism. Yet the transition was inconclusive, neither clear nor complete, and the result was a hybrid mixture that combined republican and liberal themes in a creative but uneasy collaboration."[82] Similarly, while Thomas Pangle's *The Spirit of Modern Republicanism* argues strenuously for the presence of Locke in early American political thought, it insists that "classical republican theory retains its primordial empirical foundation in the actual deeds and speeches and attitudes that continue to characterize republican statesmanship and citizenship" in the United States.[83] This synthesis of liberalism and republicanism by Lienesch and Pangle, while somewhat different from my treatment of the two theoretical strains in Jefferson's thought, nevertheless confirms the possibility of a distinctive "liberal republicanism" in early American political thought, rendering Jefferson and others more consistent and intelligible.

---

[81] Matthews, *The Radical Politics of Thomas Jefferson*, p. 11. See Appleby, *Capitalism and the New Social Order*; Daniel Boorstin, *The Lost World of Thomas Jefferson* (New York: Henry Holt, 1984); McCoy, *The Elusive Republic*; Pocock, *The Machiavellian Moment*; and Banning, *The Jeffersonian Persuasion*.

[82] Michael Lienesch, *New Order of the Ages*, (Princeton: Princeton University Press, 1988), pp. 7–8 (see my review of this book in *The American Political Science Review*, December 1989).

[83] Pangle, *The Spirit of Modern Republicanism*, p. 277.

INDEX

Adams, Henry, describing Southern culture, 118, 118n
Adams, John, on natural aristocracy, 80n
Adams, John Quincy, 94, 97–98, 108
Alien and Sedition Act, 124–25n
American Revolution: as classical republican act, 6–7; controversy over ideology of, 3–4; ideals of, 98; Jefferson's approach toward, 19
Ancient Constitution, 159, 167–68; absence of, in Declaration of Independence, 40; appeal to, during American Revolution, 6; Parliamentary appeal to, in Glorious Revolution, 23–24; relation of, to Lockean liberalism, 24–25, 30–31; use of, by Jefferson, 25–30, 36–40
Anglican church, 106, 108; and Virginia gentry culture, 115, 118, 125
Appleby, Joyce: on classical republican paradigm, 5, 156; on Jefferson, 57, 63n, 156–57
Aquinas, Thomas, Saint, 161
Arendt, Hannah, on Jefferson's political philosophy, 54n
Aristocracy, 18; Federalist, 82; natural, 17, 79–82; Tory, 82
Aristotle: on agriculture and democracy, 76n; in classical republican paradigm, 5; classical versus Tory, 159, 162; economics and politics,

73n, 75n; on equality, 78n; on ethics, 14; on happiness, 44n; on human nature, 8, 8n, 55n; on limits of size of state, 70n; on noble pleasure, 56n; on politics, 11–12, 60n, 69n; on virtue, 11, 11n, 76n

Bailyn, Bernard, 148–50
Banning, Lance, 153
Barber, Benjamin, on relation of participatory democracy and natural rights, 72n
Bill of Rights, 146
Blacks, American: Jefferson's attitudes on, 129–33; in Virginia, 139
Blackstone, Sir William, in Jefferson's journal, 27
Bolingbroke, Lord, 91n
British empire: ideology of, 22–25; Jefferson's theory of, 31–33
British liberalism. See Lockean liberalism

Capitalism: compatible with virtue in Jefferson, 63n, 154; and Lockean ethics, 14, 14n; in Virginia, 122. See Economics
Charles I, 22
Christian gentleman: characteristics of, 115–21; Jefferson as, 117n
Christianity: ethics and Jefferson, 15, 103–11, 125, 143; of Virginia gentry, 118–19. See also Church

171